System Programming with Go

Unlock the Power of System Calls, Networking, and Security with Practical Golang Projects

Tommy Clark

1

Discover other books in the series

Disclaimer

The information provided in "*System Programming with Go: Unlock the Power of System Calls, Networking, and Security with Practical Golang Projects*" by Tommy Clark is intended solely for educational and informational purposes.

While every effort has been made to ensure the accuracy and completeness of the content, the author and publisher make no guarantees regarding the results that may be achieved by following the instructions or techniques described in this book.

Readers are encouraged to seek appropriate professional guidance for specific issues or challenges they may encounter, particularly in commercial or critical environments.

The author and publisher disclaim all liability for any loss, damage, or inconvenience arising directly or indirectly from the use or misuse of the information contained within this book. Any reliance on the information provided is at the reader's own risk.

Introduction

This is "**System Programming with Go: Unlock the Power of System Calls, Networking, and Security with Practical Golang Projects**." Learning system programming is more important than ever in a time when systems need to be reliable, responsive, and secure. Go's ease of use, effectiveness, and strong concurrency features make it an ideal choice for addressing the difficulties of contemporary system-level programming.

With the help of the Go programming language, this Book seeks to close the knowledge gap between theory and experience by giving you a thorough grasp of system programming ideas. This book is designed to walk you through the intricacies of system calls, networking, and security, all wrapped up in useful, hands-on projects, regardless of whether you are an experienced developer trying to broaden your skill set or a novice keen to learn more about the field of systems programming.

You will learn the fundamentals of system programming across the chapters, starting with a strong foundation in Go. You will learn important ideas in each part, like using system calls to communicate with the operating system, creating effective network applications, and putting strong security procedures in place. We will examine how Go may be utilized to build systems that are not only operational but also exhibit remarkable performance under stress, using both practical examples and easily understandable explanations.

You will be able to apply your skills and create your own

applications by using the projects in this book as stepping stones. Every project is intended to strengthen your learning and improve your coding skills, from creating networked services to delving into the complexities of socket programming to protecting your apps from frequent vulnerabilities.

You will have a firm grasp of system programming in Go and the self-assurance to take on your own projects by the end of this book. You will have the skills required to build code that works closely with the operating system and the underlying hardware in a secure, dependable, and efficient   manner.

Come along on this thrilling adventure to discover the potential of Go system programming. Let's explore the nuances of system calls, make the most of networking, and create safe apps that can withstand the demands of the modern digital world. Now is the time to start your system programming adventure!

Chapter 1: System Programming with GoFundamentals

The field of system programming focuses on developing software that supports computer hardware. It entails creating tools and systems-level software that communicate directly with the operating system, manage resources, and control hardware. Because of their fine-grained control over system resources, languages like C and C++ have historically dominated this field; nevertheless, more contemporary languages have recently surfaced as competitors. Go, created at Google in the latter part of the 2000s, is notable for its focus on developer productivity, efficiency, and simplicity.

What Makes System Programming the Best Option?

Go, often known as Golang, has special qualities that make it ideal for system programming:

Performance: Go is a compiled language that performs similarly to C, which makes it a desirable option for system-level apps.

Concurrency Go makes it easier to create concurrent programs, which is a crucial component of contemporary system-level applications, thanks to its built-in support for concurrency via goroutines and channels.

Go's design philosophy prioritizes readability and simplicity, which helps developers maintain complicated system software.

Cross-Platform Compatibility: Go allows you to create code once and have it run everywhere because it can compile for different systems.

Garbage Collection: Low-level languages frequently have memory management issues that can be avoided with automatic memory management.

Setting Up the Go Environment

Before diving into system programming with Go, it's imperative to set up a robust development environment. Here's a step-by-step guide to getting started:

1. Install Go

You can download and install Go from the [official Go website](https://golang.org/dl/). The installation process is straightforward and includes:

Download the installer for your operating system.
Follow the prompts to install Go.
Set up your `GOPATH` and `GOROOT` environment variables as per the installation instructions. ### 2. Configure Your Development Environment
To write Go code, you'll want a good editor or integrated development environment (IDE). Popular choices include:

Visual Studio Code: A lightweight and highly extensible editor with great Go support via extensions.

GoLand: A commercial IDE specifically designed for

Go development with excellent features for system programming.

Vim/Emacs: Classic editors that can be configured with Go tools for a more hands-on codingexperience.

3. Verify the Installation

Once you've installed Go, you can verify the installation using the terminal.

```bash
go version
```

You should see the installed version of Go. You can also check that the `GOPATH` is set correctly byrunning:

```bash
echo $GOPATH
```

Basic Syntax and Features of Go

Before tackling deeper system programming concepts, let's review some fundamental features and syntax in Go.

Hello, Go!

Let's start with the classic "Hello, World!" program:

```go
package mainimport "fmt"
```

```go
func main() { fmt.Println("Hello, World!")
}
```

Data Types and Control Structures

Go features a rich set of data types, including integers, floats, strings, and booleans. Control structures like `if`, `for`, and `switch` provide the necessary flow control mechanisms.

```go
var a int = 10if a > 5 {
fmt.Println("Greater than 5")
}
```

Functions and Packages

Functions are first-class citizens in Go, and you can organize code into packages to promote modular programming.

```go
package mainimport "fmt"
// Function that adds two integersfunc add(x int, y int) int
{
return x + y
}

func main() { fmt.Println(add(3, 4))
}
```

Introduction to Goroutines and Channels

Concurrency is where Go truly shines with its built-in support for goroutines and channels. A goroutine is a lightweight thread managed by the Go runtime.

Goroutines

```go
go func() {
fmt.Println("This runs in a goroutine!")
}()
```

Channels

Channels are used to communicate between goroutines and synchronize their execution.

```go
ch := make(chan string)

go func() {
ch <- "Message from goroutine"
}()

msg := <-ch fmt.Println(msg)
```

Building Your First System Tool

Let's create a simple system tool that checks the system's

13

disk usage. This will involve executing system commands and processing their output.

Disk Usage Tool

Create a new Go file named `disk_usage.go`.

Implement the code to execute the `df` command, which displays disk space usage:

```go
package main

import ( "fmt" "os/exec""strings"
)

func main() {
// Execute the df command
out, err := exec.Command("df", "-h").Output()if err != nil
{
fmt.Println("Error executing command:", err)return
}

// Convert output bytes to string and print output :=
string(out)
lines := strings.Split(output, "\n")

for _, line := range lines {fmt.Println(line)
}
}
```

Run your tool:

14

```bash
go run disk_usage.go
```

We covered why Go is an excellent choice for system-level applications, the steps to set up your development environment, basic syntax, concurrency features, and created a simple disk usage tool. With these foundations, you're now ready to explore more advanced topics like file handling, network programming, and creating system-level utilities in Go. In subsequent chapters, we will build on these principles to delve deeper into the power and utility of Go in system programming.

The Power Go for System Programming

While high-level programming languages and frameworks often grab the spotlight, system programming operates behind the scenes, orchestrating the interactions between hardware and software, and ensuring that our devices work seamlessly. In this chapter, we will explore the essence of system programming, its key components, and its profound impact on modern computing.

1. Understanding System Programming

System programming refers to the development of system software that supports application software by providing services directly to the hardware. Unlike application programming, which focuses on solving user- centric problems, system programming aims to create a robust environment for applications to execute efficiently. The major components of system software include operating systems, device drivers, compilers, and utilities.

1.1 The Role of an Operating System

The operating system (OS) is the cornerstone of system programming. It serves as an intermediary between users and the computer hardware. The OS manages resources such as the CPU, memory, storage, and input/output devices. It provides services like process management, memory management, file systems, and security. Understanding how to program at the system level allows developers to create more efficient algorithms and optimize resource management.

1.2 Device Drivers

Device drivers are specialized software that allow the operating system to communicate with hardware peripherals. Each device, whether it's a printer, keyboard, or graphics card, requires a driver to function correctly. System programming in this context involves writing code that translates OS commands into a format that hardware can understand.

1.3 Compilers and Assemblers

Compilers and assemblers are vital components of system programming. A compiler translates high-level programming languages into machine code, while an assembler converts assembly language into executable machine code. Understanding these tools is essential for developers who wish to write efficient, low-level code and

16

optimize performance.

2. Language of Choice

System programming is commonly associated with low-level programming languages such as C, C++, and assembly language. These languages provide a closer interaction with hardware, offering low-level controland higher performance.

2.1 Why C?

C has become the dominant language for system programming due to its efficiency, portability, and close alignment with hardware. It allows developers to perform memory management and has a rich set of libraries to handle system calls. Furthermore, C serves as the foundation for many other modern languages, making it invaluable for understanding system-level operations.

2.2 C++ and Beyond

While C remained the traditional choice for system programming, C++ has introduced object-oriented paradigms that can enhance the modularity and maintainability of system software. Additionally, languages like Rust are emerging as alternatives, providing memory safety while still delivering performance close to Cand C++.

3. System Programming in Practice

System programming involves numerous practical

applications that directly impact everyday computing experiences. From embedded systems in appliances to the kernel of an operating system, system programming shapes how users interact with technology.

3.1 Embedded Systems

Embedded systems are specialized computing systems that perform dedicated functions within larger mechanical or electrical systems. System programming here involves optimizing code to run efficiently on limited hardware resources, ensuring reliability, and maintaining performance under constraints.

3.2 Kernel Development

The kernel is the core part of an OS that manages system resources. Writing kernel code requires a deep understanding of hardware operations, memory management, and process scheduling. Developers focused on kernel development often work on improving the performance, security, and scalability of operating systems.

3.3 Performance Optimization

System programming also involves performance optimization for applications. By writing efficient system-level code, developers can reduce latency, decrease resource usage, and enhance the overall responsiveness of applications. Profiling tools can help identify bottlenecks, and system programmers play a crucial role in addressing these issues.

4. The Future of System Programming

As technology evolves, so does the landscape of system programming. With the growth of cloud computing, artificial intelligence, and the Internet of Things (IoT), system programmers face new challenges and opportunities. The increased need for secure systems, efficient resource management, and robust networks highlights the enduring importance of system programming.

4.1 The Rise of Secure Programming

As cyber threats continue to evolve, secure system programming has become a critical focus. Writing code that anticipates potential vulnerabilities and protects against attacks is paramount for system programmers. Concepts such as secure coding practices, secure boot processes, and encrypted communications are becoming essential skills.

4.2 Enhancing Collaboration with Higher-Level Languages

Modern system programming increasingly involves collaboration with higher-level programming languages. Hybrid approaches allow developers to leverage the strengths of both low- and high-level languages, resulting in optimized applications that maintain safety and performance.

The power of system programming lies in its ability to

serve as the backbone of modern computing. It encompasses everything from the minutiae of hardware interaction to the overarching principles governing operating systems and resource allocation.

Key Features of Go in System-Level Development

Launched in 2009, it has gained significant traction in the realm of system-level development due to its simplicity, efficiency, and robustness. As the need for high-performance applications in an era of cloud computing and microservices architecture grows, Go has emerged as a compelling choice for system architects and developers alike. This chapter explores the key features of Go that make it particularly advantageous for system-level development.

1. Concurrency Support

One of the standout features of Go is its built-in support for concurrency, which allows developers to perform multiple operations simultaneously, making it highly suitable for networked applications and systems programming. Go's concurrency model is based on lightweight constructs called Goroutines andChannels.

Goroutines

Goroutines allow functions or methods to run independently and concurrently with other functions. They areextremely lightweight, with the ability to spawn thousands of them with minimal overhead, as they consume about 2 KB of stack space initially. This makes potentially blocking operations like I/O seamless and efficient, allowing system-level developers to build responsive applications.

Channels

Channels provide a way for Goroutines to communicate with each other and synchronize execution. They can be thought of as pipes through which data flows. Using channels helps avoid ambiguous states in concurrent programming, as the data flow can be explicitly controlled. This built-in model simplifies complex multi-threaded programming and enables safe data sharing among Goroutines.

2. Strong Typing with Type Inference

Go enforces strong static typing, which leads to type safety and prevents many classes of runtime errors. However, it also incorporates type inference, meaning that the compiler can determine the type of a variable without an explicit declaration. This blend promotes code clarity while reducing verbosity, allowing system-level developers to write clean and maintainable code.

Benefits in System-Level Development

In system-level programming, where performance and memory management are critical, strong typing allows developers to catch type-related errors at compile-time rather than at runtime. This helps in minimizing the risks of unexpected behaviors caused by incorrect data types, which can lead to critical failures in system applications.

3. Built-in Memory Management

Go includes an efficient garbage collector that manages memory automatically, alleviating developers from the manual memory management burdens characteristic of languages like C and C++.

Efficient Garbage Collection

The garbage collector in Go is designed to handle large heaps and concurrent applications effectively. It minimizes pause times and optimally manages memory allocation and deallocation. For system-level development, where resource constraints and performance are vital, Go's garbage collection offers reliability without sacrificing efficiency.

4. Simple Syntax and Comprehensive Standard Library

Go's syntax is straightforward and familiar to many developers. This simplicity encourages readability and ease of learning. Coupled with its comprehensive standard library, Go enables system-level developers to perform advanced operations, network programming, and file manipulation without needing to rely on third-party libraries excessively.

Standard Library

The Go standard library contains packages for handling common tasks such as input/output, string manipulation, and network programming. Components such as `net/http` make it easy to build web servers or clients, while `os` provides access to operating system functionality, which is essential for system-level tasks.

5. Cross-Compilation

Go's ability to compile code for different operating systems and architectures from a single codebase is a game-changer for system-level development. The Go compiler is designed to produce binaries that can run independently of the environment that built them (with the exception of configuration files or certain dynamic libraries).

Advantages of Cross-Compilation

Cross-compilation simplifies the process of deploying applications in diverse environments—a common requirement in system-level programming. Developers can write code once and compile it to run on various platforms without the overhead of maintaining separate codebases.

6. Built-in Testing Framework

Go's commitment to best practices is evident in its built-in testing framework. Integrating unit tests directly into the development cycle allows developers to validate their code easily. This native support promotes high-quality code and facilitates debugging during system-level development.

Importance of Testing in System-Level Development

In system-level development, where code complexity and system interactions can introduce subtle bugs, having a robust testing framework helps developers ensure their systems behave as expected under various conditions. Go's testing tool provides benchmarks, race condition detection, and comprehensive test coverage reporting.

Go's unique features make it a formidable language for system-level development. Its straightforward syntax, efficient concurrency model, robust standard library, and built-in tooling for testing enhance developer productivity while ensuring high performance and reliability.

Chapter 2: Understanding Go's Concurrency Model

The concurrency model of Go is built on the concept of goroutines and channels, making it easier to write programs that can handle multiple tasks simultaneously. In this chapter, we will explore the components of Go's concurrency model, how they work, and their advantages in building efficient applications.

2.1 What is Concurrency?

Before diving into Go's concurrency model, it's important to understand what concurrency means. Concurrency refers to the ability of a program to execute multiple tasks seemingly at the same time. This doesn't necessarily mean that these tasks are running simultaneously—especially on a single-core processor—but rather that they can be in progress during overlapping time periods. In contrast, parallelism refers to tasks that are executed literally at the same time, often on multiple processors or cores.

In the realm of programming, concurrency is vital in scenarios such as web servers, where thousands of client requests need to be handled simultaneously, or in applications where multiple data streams need to be processed efficiently.

2.2 Goroutines: Lightweight Threads

In Go, concurrency is primarily managed through goroutines, which are lightweight threads managed by the

Go runtime. Unlike traditional threads, goroutines are less resource-intensive and can be created quickly.
Here are some key points about goroutines:

Creation: A goroutine is initiated by using the `go` keyword followed by a function call. The function will execute concurrently with other goroutines.

```go
go myFunction()
```

Stack Management: Goroutines start with a small stack (typically 2 KB), which can grow and shrink as needed. This allows a large number of goroutines to coexist in the same application, as their memory footprint remains minimal.

Concurrency: Goroutines are multiplexed onto available system threads by the Go runtime, allowing for high concurrency levels without overwhelming the operating system.

Example of Goroutines

Here's a simple example that demonstrates the use of goroutines:

```go
package main

import ("fmt"
"time"
```

```go
)

func sayHello() {
for i := 0; i < 5; i++ { fmt.Println("Hello from goroutine")
time.Sleep(100 * time.Millisecond)
}
}

func main() {
go sayHello() // Start the goroutine

for i := 0; i < 5; i++ {
fmt.Println("Hello from main function")time.Sleep(150 *
time.Millisecond)
}
}
```

In this example, `sayHello` runs concurrently with the main function, showcasing the power of goroutines to perform tasks in parallel without complex thread management.

2.3 Channels: Communicating Between Goroutines

While goroutines allow for concurrent execution, communication between them is crucial to avoid data races and ensure consistency. Go provides a powerful mechanism for this communication through channels.

What Are Channels?

Channels are first-class types in Go that facilitate the safe exchange of data between goroutines. They operate on the principle of sending and receiving values, similar to a pipe. When one goroutine sends a value on a channel, another goroutine can receive that value, maintaining synchronization between the two.

Creating and Using Channels

To create a channel, use the `make` function with the `chan` keyword. The channel can be either bi-directional or directional (send-only or receive-only).

```go
ch := make(chan int) // Create a channel of type int
```

Here's an example of using channels:

```go
package main

import ("fmt"
)

func square(n int, ch chan int) {
ch <- n * n // Send the square of n to the channel
}

func main() {
ch := make(chan int)

for i := 0; i < 5; i++ {
go square(i, ch) // Start a goroutine for each square
```

```
calculation
}

for i := 0; i < 5; i++ {
fmt.Println(<-ch) // Receive values from the channel
}
}
```

In this code snippet, each goroutine computes the square of a number and sends the result to the main goroutine through the channel. The main function then receives and prints the results.

2.4 Synchronization with Wait Groups

In some cases, it's necessary to wait for multiple goroutines to complete before proceeding. This is where WaitGroups come in handy. A `sync.WaitGroup` provides a straightforward way to wait for a collection of goroutines to finish executing.

Using Wait Groups

You can add the number of goroutines to wait for using `Add`, mark them as done using `Done`, and wait for completion using `Wait`:

```go
package main

import ("fmt"
"sync"
```

```
)

func printNumbers(wg *sync.WaitGroup, n int) { defer
wg.Done() // Notify that this goroutine is done
fmt.Println(n)
}

func main() {
var wg sync.WaitGroup

for i := 0; i < 5; i++ {
wg.Add(1) // Add one goroutine to the WaitGroup go
printNumbers(&wg, i)
}

wg.Wait() // Wait for all goroutines to finish
}
```
```

In this example, the `main` function initializes a
WaitGroup, adds goroutines, and waits for their
completionbefore exiting.

## 2.5 Handling Concurrency in Real-world Applications

Go's concurrency model is a perfect fit for building
scalable applications, especially microservices and web
servers. By leveraging goroutines and channels,
developers can create efficient services that handle
numerous requests, carry out asynchronous operations,
and process streams of data effortlessly.

However, it is essential to design with concurrency in
```

mind to avoid issues like deadlocks, race conditions, and resource starvation. To mitigate these risks, Go provides tools for debugging concurrent programs, including the race detector.

Go's concurrency model, characterized by goroutines and channels, provides developers with powerful tools to create highly concurrent programs with relative ease. The lightweight nature of goroutines enables developers to handle thousands of concurrent tasks without the overhead traditionally associated with threading models.

In this chapter, we explored the fundamentals of Go's concurrency model, including goroutines, channels, synchronization with WaitGroups, and practical considerations for real-world applications. Understanding these concepts will empower you to write efficient, concurrent code, enabling you to tackle complex programming challenges effectively.

Introduction to Goroutines and Channels

Developed at Google, Go was designed to simplify the complexities of software construction, especially in a world increasingly characterized by distributed systems and parallel processing. This chapter will introduce you to two of Go's foundational concurrency primitives: Goroutines and Channels, which allow developers to build highly concurrent applications with ease and elegance.

The Need for Concurrency

As applications grow in complexity, so does the need for performing multiple tasks simultaneously. Traditional single-threaded programming models can lead to inefficiencies, especially when handling I/O-bound tasks, such as network requests, database queries, or file operations. In such cases, leveraging concurrency allows developers to maximize resource utilization, improve performance, and create a more responsive user experience.

Concurrency enables different parts of a program to execute independently while possibly communicating with each other. In Go, this is implemented primarily through Goroutines and Channels, which reduce the complexity of managing multiple threads and their interactions.

What Are Goroutines?

A Goroutine is a lightweight thread managed by Go's runtime. Launching a Goroutine is as simple as using the `go` keyword followed by a function call. This abstraction allows you to execute functions asynchronously without the heavy overhead of managing OS threads directly.

Example of Using a Goroutine

Here is a simple example of how to create and run a Goroutine:

```go
package main
```

```go
import ("fmt"
"time"
)

func sayHello() {
for i := 0; i < 5; i++ { fmt.Println("Hello from
Goroutine!")time.Sleep(100 * time.Millisecond)
}
}

func main() {
go sayHello() // Launching a Goroutine
// The main function will continue executingfor i := 0; i <
5; i++ {
fmt.Println("Hello    from    Main!")    time.Sleep(150    *
time.Millisecond)
}

}
```

In this example, the `sayHello` function is called as a Goroutine. This means the main function can continue to execute independently, leading to concurrent output. The concurrency model in Go allows multiple Goroutines to share the same address space, which makes communication and data sharing efficient.

What Are Channels?

While Goroutines handle the execution of concurrent tasks, Channels are a built-in mechanism for communication between those Goroutines. Channels

33

allow one Goroutine to send data to another, enabling safe data transfer and synchronization.

Channels in Go are typed, meaning that they can only send and receive a specific data type. This type safety provides clarity and prevents many runtime errors associated with type mismatches.

Creating and Using Channels

Channels are created using the `make` function, and data can be sent and received using the `<-` operator. Here's an example demonstrating how to use Channels:
```go
package main

import ("fmt"
)

func square(n int, ch chan int) {
ch <- n * n // Send the square of n to the channel
}

func main() {
ch := make(chan int) // Creating a channel for i := 1; i <= 5; i++ {
go square(i, ch) // Launching a Goroutine to compute square
}
// Receiving values from the channel for i := 1; i <= 5; i++
{
fmt.Println("Square:", <-ch)
}
```

```
}
```

In this code snippet, we define a `square` function that sends the square of a number to a Channel. In the `main` function, we launch multiple Goroutines to compute squares concurrently, and we collect the results through the channel.

Goroutines and Channels form the backbone of Go's concurrency model, allowing developers to buildsystems that are fast, efficient, and easy to reason about.

Managing Data Races and Synchronization

In this chapter, we'll explore strategies for managing data races and ensuring effective synchronization inGo.

Understanding Data Races

Before diving into prevention and synchronization techniques, it's crucial to understand what a data race is.A data race occurs when:

Two or more goroutines access the same variable concurrently.
At least one of the accesses is a write.

This situation can result in inconsistent and unexpected results. For example, suppose one goroutine is updating a shared counter while another is reading its value. Without proper synchronization, the reader might get a stale or incomplete value.

Identifying Data Races

Go provides a built-in race detector to help identify data races during development. To use the race detector, compile and run your program with the `-race` flag:

```bash
go run -race your_program.go
```

When the race detector finds a race condition, it will output a detailed message indicating where the conflict occurred. While this tool is invaluable, it should be used during the development phase, as running with the race detector can slightly slow down your program's performance.

Synchronization Techniques

Go provides several mechanisms to manage synchronization and prevent data races: ### 1. Mutexes
The most common way to manage access to shared data is through the use of `sync.Mutex`. A mutex (short for mutual exclusion) allows only one goroutine to access the critical section of code at a time.

```go
package main

import (
"fmt"
```

```go
    "sync"
)

var (
counter int
mu      sync.Mutex
wg      sync.WaitGroup
)

func increment() {defer wg.Done()
mu.Lock()   // Lock the mutex counter++     // Critical
section mu.Unlock()              // Unlock the mutex
}

func main() {
for i := 0; i < 1000; i++ {wg.Add(1)
go increment()


}
```
```
}
wg.Wait()
fmt.Println("Final Counter:", counter)
```

In this example, we use a `sync.Mutex` to lock the critical section where we modify the `counter`. This approach ensures that only one goroutine can increment the counter at a time, preventing data races.

2. RWMutex

If you have a scenario where reads are more frequent than writes, `sync.RWMutex` might be more appropriate. This allows multiple goroutines to read from shared data concurrently but ensures exclusive access for writing.

```go
package main

import (
"fmt"
"sync"
)

var (
counter int
mu      sync.RWMutex wg  sync.WaitGroup
)

func readCounter() {defer wg.Done()
mu.RLock() //     Lock    in    a    read    mode
fmt.Println("Counter:", counter) // Read operation
mu.RUnlock()              // Unlock the read lock
}

func increment() {defer wg.Done()
mu.Lock()   // Lock in a write mode counter++      //
Critical section mu.Unlock()            // Unlock the
write lock
```

```go
}

func main() {
for i := 0; i < 1000; i++ {wg.Add(1)
go increment()
}
for i := 0; i < 10; i++ {wg.Add(1)
go readCounter()


}
```

}
wg.Wait()
fmt.Println("Final Counter:", counter)

In this code snippet, we utilize `sync.RWMutex` for optimal reading and writing access. Multiple readers can access the counter concurrently as long as no goroutine is writing to it.

3. Channels

Go's channels are a powerful way to synchronize goroutines. Instead of sharing data between goroutines, you can use channels to communicate values safely.

```go
package main

import (
"fmt"
```

```go
)

func main() {
ch := make(chan int)

go func() {
for i := 0; i < 1000; i++ {
ch <- i // Send value to the channel
}
close(ch) // Close the channel
}()

for val := range ch { // Receive values until the channel is
closedfmt.Println(val)
}
}
```

Using channels eliminates the need for explicit locks, as they ensure that only one goroutine accesses the data at a time when sending or receiving.

4. Atomic Operations

For certain types of shared data, especially simple counters, you can use the `sync/atomic` package, which provides low-level atomic operations. This approach can be more efficient than using mutexes for simple usecases.

```go
package main

import (
```

```go
"fmt"
"sync" "sync/atomic"
)

var counter int64
var wg sync.WaitGroup

func increment() {defer wg.Done()
atomic.AddInt64(&counter, 1) // Atomically increment
the counter
}

func main() {
for i := 0; i < 1000; i++ {wg.Add(1)
go increment()



}
```
```
}
wg.Wait()
fmt.Println("Final Counter:", counter)
```

In this example, `atomic.AddInt64` is used to increment `counter` without needing a mutex. This can enhance performance by reducing lock contention.

Data races can lead to elusive bugs that are difficult to detect and fix. However, Go provides robust tools for managing concurrency and synchronization, including mutexes, channels, and atomic operations.
Understanding and implementing these techniques is crucial for building safe, efficient, and concurrent

applications in Go.

Chapter 3: System Calls in Go

This chapter delves into the concept of system calls in the context of the Go programming language, exploring how Go interfaces with the underlying system, how to make system calls, and the best practices for using them effectively.

3.1 Understanding System Calls

System calls are essential functions that allow user space applications to interact with hardware resources through the kernel. They provide a controlled interface to perform operations like file management, process control, and network communication, typically abstracting the complexities of the underlying hardware.

In Go, system calls are not directly called like in lower-level languages such as C. Instead, Go provides a rich standard library that wraps around these system calls. Functions in the standard library internally convert these calls into suitable system call parameters and handle the intricacies involved.

3.2 The Role of the `syscall` Package

Go provides the `syscall` package, which offers a low-level interface to the operating system's system calls. This package contains functions that allow you to perform tasks that usually require explicit system calls, such as file operations, networking, and process management.

Here's a brief overview of what you can do using the

`syscall` package:

File Operations: Open, read, write, and close files.
Process Management: Forking processes, executing new programs, and managing process IDs.
Networking: Creating sockets, binding, listening, and accepting connections.

In general, however, it is recommended to use the higher-level packages from the Go standard library, such as `os`, `net`, and `os/exec`, as they provide more robust error handling and are easier to use.

3.3 Example: Making File System Calls

Let's explore how to make basic file system calls in Go using the `os` package, which internally utilizes system calls to interact with files. Below is an example illustrating how to create, write to, and read from a file:

```go
package main

import ("fmt"
"os"
)

func main() {
// Create a new file
file, err := os.Create("example.txt")if err != nil {
fmt.Println("Error creating file:", err)return

}
```

```go
defer file.Close()

// Write to the file
_, err = file.WriteString("Hello, Go System Calls!")if err !=
nil {
fmt.Println("Error writing to file:", err)return
}

// Open the file for reading
file, err = os.Open("example.txt")if err != nil {
fmt.Println("Error opening file:", err)return
}
defer file.Close()

// Read from the file
data := make([]byte, 64) // buffer to hold the read data
bytesRead, err := file.Read(data)
if err != nil {
fmt.Println("Error reading from file:", err)return
}

fmt.Printf("Read          from          file:          %s\n",
string(data[:bytesRead]))
}
```

In this example, we create a file named "example.txt", write a string to it, and then read the content back. The underlying calls to open, write, and read are translated by the Go runtime into system calls, handling all the necessary details so developers can focus on application logic.

3.4 Handling Errors

One significant aspect of system calls is error handling. When dealing with system-dependent code, errors must be interpreted correctly. Go's error handling philosophy promotes returning errors as values, allowing developers to manage them effectively. Always check for errors after invoking methods that perform systemcalls to ensure that your application behaves as expected.

3.5 Using `golang.org/x/sys` for Advanced System Calls

For more advanced functionality and system calls not covered in the standard library, the `golang.org/x/sys` package provides additional support. This package contains low-level API bindings, exposing many system calls and additional features from Unix-like operating systems.

Here's an example of how to use the `golang.org/x/sys/unix` package to change file permissions:

```go
package main

import ( "golang.org/x/sys/unix"

"os"
)

func main() {
```

```
err := os.Chmod("example.txt", 0755)if err != nil {
fmt.Println("Error changing permissions:", err)return
}

// Alternatively, using the unix package err =
unix.Chmod("example.txt", 0755)if err != nil {
fmt.Println("Error changing permissions with unix
package:", err)return
}
}
` ` `
```

In this code, we demonstrate how to change the file permissions of "example.txt" using both the `os` and `unix` packages.

3.6 Best Practices

Favor Higher-Level Abstractions: Whenever possible, utilize higher-level libraries provided by Go. They typically offer better error handling, safety, and functionality.
Check for Errors: Always validate the error returned from system call wrappers to avoid unexpectedapplication behavior.
Optimize for Portability: Since system calls can vary between operating systems, keep this in mind when writing cross-platform applications. Use conditional compilation or interfaces when necessary to abstract away platform-specific details.

System calls form the backbone of interaction between Go applications and the operating system. While the `syscall` package offers powerful features, relying on the standard library provides a more developer- friendly and robust approach to system interactions. Understanding how to leverage these tools effectively is crucial for building efficient and reliable applications in Go.

Making System Calls in Go

In the Go programming language, system calls allow developers to tap into low-level operating system features and resources while maintaining Go's simplicity and safety. This chapter will demystify system calls in Go, exploring how to use them effectively and safely, and providing practical examples.

Understanding System Calls

A system call is a mechanism by which a program requests a service from the kernel of the operating system.Common examples of system calls include reading from or writing to files, creating or terminating processes, and managing system resources like memory and CPU time. In Go, interacting with these system calls can be somewhat abstracted; however, understanding the underlying concepts is crucial for writing efficient and effective Go applications.

The Go Standard Library

Before diving into raw system calls, it's essential to recognize that Go's standard library provides many high-level abstractions that wrap around system calls. For example, the `os` and `net` packages offer extensive functionality for file handling and networking without directly calling the operating system's APIs. It is often advisable to use these packages unless you need specific features not covered by the standard library.

Example of High-Level File Operations

Here's a simple example of reading a file using Go's `os` package:

```go
package main

import ( "fmt" "io/ioutil""log"
)

func main() {
data, err := ioutil.ReadFile("example.txt")if err != nil {
log.Fatal(err)
}
fmt.Println(string(data))
}
```

In this example, the `ReadFile` function wraps system calls related to opening, reading, and closing a file, demonstrating how Go abstracts the complexities of system calls in many common scenarios.

Making Raw System Calls

In some advanced scenarios, you might need to execute raw system calls directly. Go provides a package called `golang.org/x/sys/unix` that allows you to access a variety of operating system calls on Unix-like systems. The package includes a wide array of constants, types, and functions that mirror Unix system calls.

Example of a System Call: Getting Process Information

Let's look at how to get information about the current process using a system call. We will use the `unix.Getpid()` function to retrieve the process ID:

```go
package main

import ("fmt"
"golang.org/x/sys/unix"
)

func main() {
pid, err := unix.Getpid()if err != nil {
fmt.Println("Error getting PID:", err)return
}
fmt.Printf("Current Process ID: %d\n", pid)
}
```

This code snippet demonstrates how to import the `unix` package and call `Getpid()` to retrieve the process ID. Handling errors here is crucial since system calls can fail for various reasons.

Error Handling in System Calls

Error handling is a crucial concern when making system calls. Unlike higher-level abstractions that might propagate errors in a controlled manner, system calls can fail and return error codes or nil. It is essential to check these error values to ensure the program can handle failures gracefully.

Example of Error Handling

Consider a scenario in which we want to open a file using the `unix.Open()` system call:

```go
package main

import ("fmt"
"golang.org/x/sys/unix"
)

func main() {
fd, err := unix.Open("example.txt", unix.O_RDONLY, o)if err != nil {
fmt.Println("Error opening file:", err)return
}
defer unix.Close(fd)

// Process the file as needed...
fmt.Println("File opened successfully, file descriptor:", fd)

}
```

In this example, the program attempts to open a file and

uses error handling to respond to potential errors in the call. This approach ensures robust and reliable code.

Advanced System Calls

As you become more comfortable with making system calls in Go, you may want to explore more advanced features. Some additional topics worth investigating include:

Inter-Process Communication (IPC): Techniques such as message passing using Unix domain sockets or signal handling to manage communication between processes.

File Descriptors and Resource Management: Managing file descriptors effectively, including the use of `select` for multiplexing I/O operations.

Concurrency and Non-blocking Calls: Taking advantage of Go's goroutines and channels to make concurrent system calls and handle I/O without blocking.

Low-level Networking: Using system calls for raw socket programming to create custom protocols or perform tasks that aren't easily served by higher-level abstractions.

Example of Non-Blocking I/O

To illustrate concurrency, let's create a simple program that reads from two files concurrently. The `goroutine` will allow each file read to occur in parallel:

```go
package main

import ( "fmt" "io/ioutil""log"
"sync"
)

func readFile(filename string, wg *sync.WaitGroup) {
defer wg.Done()
data, err := ioutil.ReadFile(filename)if err != nil {
log.Println("Error reading file:", err)return
}
fmt.Printf("Contents of %s:\n%s\n", filename,
string(data))
}

func main() {
var wg sync.WaitGroup
files := []string{"file1.txt", "file2.txt"}

for _, file := range files {wg.Add(1)

go readFile(file, &wg)
}

wg.Wait()
}
```

This code uses `sync.WaitGroup` to manage concurrency effectively, allowing multiple files to be read without blocking the main thread.

While Go provides a rich and powerful standard library that abstracts many of these complexities, system calls remain an important tool in a developer's toolkit. By understanding how to use the `golang.org/x/sys/unix` package and the principles of error handling, concurrency, and resource management, you can build efficient and robust applications that leverage the power of the operating system while embracing Go's simplicity and elegance.

Handling Errors from System Calls in Go

In systems programming, interacting with the operating system often involves making system calls to perform essential functions such as file manipulation, network communication, and process control. While Go provides a convenient abstraction over these system calls, understanding how to handle errors effectively is crucial to writing robust and reliable applications. In this chapter, we will explore how to handle errors from system calls in Go, with practical examples and best practices.

Understanding Errors in Go

Go adopts a simple yet powerful approach to error handling by utilizing multiple return values. Wherever an error can occur, functions return a value that represents success (or the resultant value) and an error value indicating whether the operation was successful or not. If the error value is `nil`, it represents a successful operation; otherwise, it contains information about what went wrong.

The `error` Type

The `error` type in Go is a built-in interface that represents an error condition. It has a single method:

```go
type error interface {Error() string
}
```

Whenever a function returns an error, it generally returns an instance of a type that implements this interface, allowing developers to inspect error messages and handle them accordingly.

Making System Calls in Go

Go's standard library encapsulates many system calls, providing a higher-level interface that often abstracts away the complexity of direct interaction with the OS. Some examples include file operations, network connections, and process management.

```go
file, err := os.Open("example.txt")if err != nil {
log.Fatalf("Failed to open file: %v", err)
}
```

In the above example, the `os.Open` function attempts to open a file, returning an error if it fails. Instead of panicking, the code gracefully handles the error, printing a message and terminating the program.

Error Handling Techniques

When handling errors from system calls in Go, several techniques can help you manage them effectively. ### 1. Checking for Errors Immediately It's essential to check for errors immediately after a system call. This practice prevents errors from propagating through the code and helps you maintain control over the execution flow.

```go
file, err := os.Open("example.txt")if err != nil {
log.Printf("Error opening file: %v", err)return
}
defer file.Close()
```

2. Providing Context

Leveraging the `fmt.Errorf` function allows you to add contextual information to errors. By wrapping errors with additional context, you enhance the ability to debug problems.

```go
file, err := os.Open("example.txt")if err != nil {
return fmt.Errorf("failed to open example.txt: %w", err)
}
```

Using the `%w` format verb in `fmt.Errorf` allows you to

later perform error inspections using `errors.Is` or `errors.As`.

3. Custom Error Types

Creating custom error types is useful when you want to convey specific information about an error condition. This practice allows you to implement additional methods and fields to propagate more context about the error.

```go
type FileError struct {Filename string
Err     error
}

func (e *FileError) Error() string {
return fmt.Sprintf("error with file %s: %v", e.Filename, e.Err)
}
```

In this case, a `FileError` can contain the file name and the underlying error, facilitating better handling. ### 4. Logging Errors
Logging errors helps maintain the health of your application and provides insights for debugging. Use the `log` package to record errors at appropriate levels (e.g., Info, Warning, Error).

```go
if err != nil {
log.Printf("Error occurred: %v", err)
```

```go
}
```

5. Retrying on Temporary Errors

For operations that may fail intermittently, such as network calls or file access, implementing a retry mechanism can improve resilience. For example:

```go
var err error
for i := 0; i < 3; i++ {
file, err = os.Open("example.txt")if err == nil {
break
}
if temporary, ok := err.(net.Error); ok && temporary.Temporary() { log.Printf("Temporary error, retrying... (%d)", i+1) time.Sleep(time.Second)
continue
}
log.Fatalf("Failed to open file after retries: %v", err)
}
defer file.Close()
```

Best Practices for Handling System Call Errors

To ensure your application handles errors from system calls effectively, consider the following best practices:

Check Errors Immediately: Always check for errors right after the function call.
Use Error Wrapping: Provide context to errors using

wrapping techniques.

Define Custom Errors: For more complex error scenarios, use custom error types.

Log Errors Appropriately: Ensure that errors are logged with enough context to aid debugging.

Consider Recovery and Retrying: Implement retry logic for transient errors where applicable.

Use Standard Error Handling Patterns: Familiarize yourself with idiomatic error handling patterns in Go, such as returning errors from functions.

By understanding how to utilize Go's error handling capabilities effectively, you can improve the reliability of your software, making it easier to maintain and debug. Throughout this chapter, we explored fundamental principles, error-checking patterns, and best practices for managing errors resulting from system calls, laying a strong foundation for error handling in Go programming. As you continue to develop your Go applications, keep these guidelines in mind, and your code will be both resilient and maintainable.

Chapter 4: File and Directory Operations

Understanding how to manipulate files and directories programmatically is crucial for any aspiring system programmer. This chapter delves into the operations associated with files and directories, emphasizing the techniques and tools necessary for effective system programming.

4.1 Overview of File Systems

A file system is a structure that allows data to be stored, organized, accessed, and managed on storage devices. Different operating systems provide various types of file systems, each with its own characteristics.Common file systems include NTFS (used by Windows), ext4 (commonly used in Linux), and HFS+ (used by macOS).

4.1.1 Components of a File System

The major components of a file system include:

Files: The individual units of storage that contain data.
Directories: Special files that provide a means to organize and manage files hierarchically.
Metadata: Information about files and directories, such as creation date, size, permissions, andownership.
Inodes: Data structures that store information about files in Unix-like systems. Understanding these components is crucial for performing file and directory

operations.## 4.2 File Operations

In the context of system programming, various operations can be performed on files. These operations can be categorized into several essential functions:

4.2.1 Creating and Deleting Files

Creating and deleting files is fundamental to file management. In C, this can be done using functions from the `stdio.h` and `unistd.h` libraries:

```c
#include <stdio.h>  #include <stdlib.h>  #include <unistd.h>

int main() {
// Create a new file
FILE *file = fopen("example.txt", "w");if (file == NULL) {
perror("Failed to create file");return EXIT_FAILURE;
}
fprintf(file, "Hello, World!\n");fclose(file);

// Delete the created file
if (remove("example.txt") != 0) {perror("Failed to delete file"); return EXIT_FAILURE;
}

return EXIT_SUCCESS;
}
```

4.2.2 Reading and Writing Files

The ability to read from and write to files is the cornerstone of file operations. The C programming languageprovides various functions for this:

```c
#include <stdio.h> #include <stdlib.h>

int main() {
FILE *file = fopen("example.txt", "r");

if (file == NULL) {
perror("Failed to open file for reading"); return EXIT_FAILURE;
}

char buffer[255];
while (fgets(buffer, sizeof(buffer), file) != NULL) {
printf("%s", buffer);
}

fclose(file);
return EXIT_SUCCESS;
}
```

The example assumes that `example.txt` was created previously. The program opens the file in read mode,reads each line until EOF, and prints it to the console.

4.2.3 File Metadata Operations

In addition to reading and writing data, it is crucial for system programmers to interact with the file metadata.

The `stat` structure in C can be utilized to retrieve information about a file:

```c
#include <sys/stat.h> #include <stdio.h> #include <stdlib.h>

int main() {
struct stat fileStat;

if (stat("example.txt", &fileStat) < 0) {

perror("Could not retrieve file information"); return EXIT_FAILURE;
}

printf("File Size: %ld bytes\n", fileStat.st_size);
printf("Number of Links: %ld\n", fileStat.st_nlink);
printf("File Permissions: %o\n", fileStat.st_mode & 0777);

return EXIT_SUCCESS;
}
```

This program retrieves and displays the size, link count, and permissions of `example.txt`. ## 4.3 Directory Operations
Directories are essential for organizing files on a file system. Just as there are operations for files, corresponding operations exist for directories.

4.3.1 Creating and Deleting Directories

Creating and deleting directories is accomplished using `mkdir` and `rmdir` functions:

```c
#include <sys/stat.h> #include <unistd.h> #include <stdio.h> #include <stdlib.h>

int main() {
// Create a new directory
if (mkdir("new_directory", 0755) != 0) {perror("Failed to create directory"); return EXIT_FAILURE;
}

// Delete the created directory
if (rmdir("new_directory") != 0) { perror("Failed to delete directory");return EXIT_FAILURE;
}

return EXIT_SUCCESS;
}
```

4.3.2 Enumerating Directories

Often, it is necessary to enumerate the contents of a directory. In C, this can be achieved using the `dirent.h` library:

```c
#include <stdio.h> #include <stdlib.h>
```

```c
#include <dirent.h>

int main() {
struct dirent *de; // Pointer for directory entry DIR *dr =
opendir(".");

if (dr == NULL) {
perror("Could not open current directory"); return
EXIT_FAILURE;
}

while ((de = readdir(dr)) != NULL) { printf("%s\n", de-
>d_name);
}

closedir(dr);
return EXIT_SUCCESS;
}
```

This example opens the current directory and lists all entries within it, including files and subdirectories. ## 4.4 Error Handling
Error handling is a critical aspect of system programming. In file and directory operations, various factors can lead to errors, including permission issues, non-existent files, and insufficient memory. Utilizing `perror` and return codes can provide meaningful feedback to users and developers.

4.4.1 Using `perror`

The `perror` function can be employed to print error messages related to system calls and library functions. It automatically uses the global variable `errno` to indicate what went wrong during the last operation.

File and directory operations are crucial components of system programming, offering a pathway to interact meaningfully with the underlying operating system. By mastering these concepts and functions, programmers can create robust applications that utilize the file system efficiently. As we progress, we will explore advanced topics like file locking, asynchronous I/O, and the role of file systems in networking, further enhancing our understanding of system programming.

Reading and Writing Files in Go

This chapter will cover the essentials of file handling in Go, including how to read from and write to files. We will explore various methods, error handling, and best practices while using file I/O in Go.

1. Introduction to File Handling in Go

Go provides the `os` and `io/ioutil` packages for file operations. The `os` package offers low-level operations, while `io/ioutil` provides simpler, higher-level functions. As you delve into file handling, you will also encounter the `bufio` and `encoding` packages, which can enhance your file I/O tasks, especially when dealing with structured data formats like JSON.

Key Topics Covered in This Chapter:
Opening files
Reading files

Writing files
Error handling
Closing files
Working with buffered I/O

2. Opening and Closing Files

Before we can read or write data, we need to open a file. The `os` package provides the `Open` function to open files for reading and the `OpenFile` function to open them with more options (like writing or appending).

Example: Opening a File

```go
package main

import ("fmt"
"os"
)

func main() {
// Open a file for reading
file, err := os.Open("example.txt")if err != nil {
fmt.Println("Error:", err)return
}
defer file.Close() // Ensuring that the file is closed after we are done fmt.Println("File opened successfully:", file.Name())
}
```

In this snippet, we attempt to open a file named

`example.txt`. If successful, we defer closing the file until the `main` function finishes, ensuring resource cleanup.

3. Reading Files

Reading All Contents

For straightforward tasks, the `ioutil` package provides a convenient `ReadFile` function to read the entire file at once.

```go
package main

import ( "fmt" "io/ioutil"
)

func main() {
data, err := ioutil.ReadFile("example.txt")if err != nil {
fmt.Println("Error:", err)return
}
fmt.Println("File Contents:")
fmt.Println(string(data)) // Converting bytes to string for display
}
```

Reading Line by Line

For more control, such as processing files line by line, we can use the `bufio` package.

```go
```

```go
package main

import ( "bufio""fmt"
"os"
)

func main() {
file, err := os.Open("example.txt")if err != nil {
fmt.Println("Error:", err)return
}
defer file.Close()

scanner := bufio.NewScanner(file)for scanner.Scan() {
fmt.Println(scanner.Text())
}
if err := scanner.Err(); err != nil { fmt.Println("Error
reading the file:", err)
}

}
```
```

The `bufio.Scanner` provides a method `Scan` that reads
the file line-by-line, allowing us to process each line
individually.

## 4. Writing Files

Just as reading can be done in various ways, writing to
files also has multiple options. The simplest methoduses
`ioutil.WriteFile`, which writes byte slices directly.

### Example: Writing to a File

69
```

```go
package main

import ( "fmt" "io/ioutil"
)

func main() {
content := []byte("Hello, Go file writing!")
err := ioutil.WriteFile("output.txt", content, 0644)if err !=
nil {
fmt.Println("Error:", err)return
}
fmt.Println("File written successfully!")
}
```

Appending to a File

To append content rather than overwrite it, the `os`
package's `OpenFile` function is useful.

```go
package main

import ("fmt"
"os"
)

func main() {
file,        err        :=        os.OpenFile("output.txt",
os.O_APPEND|os.O_WRONLY, 0644)if err != nil {
fmt.Println("Error:", err)return
```

```go
}
defer file.Close()

if _, err := file.WriteString("\nAppending new line!"); err
!= nil {fmt.Println("Error:", err)

} else {
fmt.Println("File updated successfully!")
}
}
```

In this example, we open the file in append mode and write a new line of content. The bitwise OR (`|`) operator is used to combine the `os.O_APPEND` and `os.O_WRONLY` flags.

5. Error Handling

Error handling is an essential part of file I/O. Many file operations can fail for various reasons (e.g., file not found, permission issues). It's good practice to always check for errors and handle them gracefully.

```go
package main

import ("fmt"
"os"
)

func safeOpen(filename string) (*os.File, error) {file, err
:= os.Open(filename)
```

```
if err != nil {
return  nil, fmt.Errorf("unable to open file %s: %w",
filename, err)
}
return file, nil
}
```

Here, we define a utility function to open a file safely. If an error occurs, we wrap it with additional context using `fmt.Errorf`.

6. Best Practices

Always Close Files: Use the `defer` keyword right after opening a file to ensure it is closed properly.
Error Handling: Always handle errors to make your code robust and user-friendly.
Use Buffered I/O: For performance-sensitive applications, consider using buffered I/O (with `bufio`)to optimize read and write operations.
File Permissions: When creating or writing files, pay attention to file permissions to maintain security.

File handling in Go is a powerful but straightforward process. With just a few functions from the standard library, you can read from and write to files efficiently. Remember to practice good error handling and resource management to ensure that your applications are reliable and maintainable. In the next chapter, we will explore more advanced topics concerning file formats and data serialization in Go.

Managing Directories and Permissions in Go

In Go, the powerful standard library provides extensive support for managing directories and their associated permissions. This chapter will walk you through creating, modifying, and managing directories, as well as setting and checking permissions.

Understanding Go's File System Interfaces

Go's I/O operations are primarily defined in the `os` and `io/ioutil` packages. These packages provide a rich set of functions to manage directories and their permissions. Familiarizing yourself with these packages is crucial for effective file system management in your applications.

Key Functions and Types

os.Mkdir: Creates a new directory with the specified name and permission mode.
os.MkdirAll: Similar to `Mkdir`, but it creates the entire path, along with any necessary parents.
os.Open: Opens a directory for reading.
os.Stat: Retrieves the file or directory information, including permissions and timestamps.
os.Chmod: Changes the permission mode of a file or directory.
os.Remove: Deletes a file or directory. ## Creating Directories
Creating a directory in Go is straightforward. The `os.Mkdir` function is used to create a single directory, while `os.MkdirAll` can create nested directories if they

do not exist.

Example of Creating a Directory

```go
package main

import ("fmt"
"os"
)

func main() {
dirName := "exampleDir"
err := os.Mkdir(dirName, 0755) // permission: rwxr-xr-x
if err != nil {
fmt.Println("Error creating directory:", err)return
}
fmt.Println("Directory created successfully:", dirName)
}
```

Creating Nested Directories

If you need to create nested directories, `os.MkdirAll` is your friend:

```go
package main

import ("fmt"
"os"
)
```

```go
func main() {
nestedDir := "parentDir/childDir"
err := os.MkdirAll(nestedDir, 0755) // permission: rwxr-
xr-xif err != nil {
fmt.Println("Error creating nested directories:", err)
return
}
fmt.Println("Nested directories created successfully:",
nestedDir)
}
```

Checking Directory Existence and Permissions

Before performing operations on directories, it is often useful to check whether they exist and to inspect their permissions. This can be achieved using `os.Stat`.

Example of Checking Directory Existence

```go
package main

import ("fmt"
"os"
)

func main() {
dirName := "exampleDir" info, err := os.Stat(dirName)if os.IsNotExist(err) {
fmt.Println("Directory does not exist.")
} else if err != nil {
fmt.Println("Error checking directory:", err)
```

```go
} else if info.IsDir() {
fmt.Println("Directory            exists.            Permission:",
info.Mode().Perm())
}
}
```

Changing Permissions

Changing the permissions of a directory is done using the `os.Chmod` function. Permissions are represented as `os.FileMode` values.

Example of Changing Permissions

```go
package main

import ("fmt"
"os"
)

func main() {
dirName := "exampleDir"
err := os.Chmod(dirName, 0700) // permission: rwx------
if err != nil {
fmt.Println("Error changing directory permissions:", err)
return
}
fmt.Println("Directory            permissions            changed
successfully.")
}
```

Deleting Directories

To remove a directory, you can use the `os.Remove` function. Note that the directory must be empty; if it contains files or subdirectories, you'll need to delete them first.

Example of Deleting a Directory

```go
package main

import ("fmt"
"os"
)

func main() {
dirName := "exampleDir" err := os.Remove(dirName) if err != nil {
fmt.Println("Error deleting directory:", err)return
}
fmt.Println("Directory deleted successfully.")
}
```

Managing directories and permissions in Go is an essential skill for any developer working with file systems. With just a few functions, you can create, check, modify, and delete directories, ensuring that your application maintains the necessary file structure and adheres to security protocols of access control.

In this chapter, we covered key operations such as creating directories, changing permissions, and deleting directories. These skills are foundational for building applications that interact with the file system efficiently and securely.

Chapter 5: Working with System Events

In this chapter, we delve into how the GO programming language can interface with system events—an aspect that enables developers to create responsive applications that react to changes in the environment. We will cover how to set up event listeners, handle triggered events, and apply these concepts in practical applications.

5.1 Understanding System Events

Before diving into coding, it's important to grasp what system events are. In essence, system events are notifications generated by the operating system or environment, prompting applications to respond to certain actions or states. These can include:

File system changes (e.g., file creation, modification, or deletion)
User actions (e.g., mouse clicks, keyboard inputs)
Network status changes (e.g., connection established or lost)

By responding to these events, applications can be more intuitive and efficient, providing users with a seamless experience.

5.2 Setting Up Your GO Environment

To work with system events in GO, ensure that you have the latest version of GO installed. If you haven't set up a GO environment yet or need a refresher, follow these steps:

Download and Install GO: Visit the [official GO website](https://golang.org/dl/) and download the latest version.

Set Up Your Workspace: Create a directory for your GO projects, and set the GOPATH environment variable accordingly.

IDE or Text Editor: Choose an IDE like Visual Studio Code, GoLand, or simply a text editor of your choice that supports GO.

Create a New GO Project: Navigate to your workspace directory and create a new folder for your project:
```shell
mkdir MyEventProjectcd MyEventProject
```

Initialize Your GO Module: Initialize a new module to manage dependencies:
```shell
go mod init MyEventProject
```

5.3 Using Third-Party Libraries for Event Handling

While GO has formidable standard libraries, some tasks, including system event handling, may rely on third-party libraries. In this section, we will utilize the `fsnotify` library for file system events.

5.3.1 Installing fsnotify

To handle file system notifications, we need to install the `fsnotify` package. Run the following command in your project root:

```shell
go get github.com/fsnotify/fsnotify
```

5.3.2 Listening for File System Events

Let's create a basic program that monitors a directory and reports changes. Create a file named `main.go` and add the following code:

```go
package main

import ("fmt"
"log" "github.com/fsnotify/fsnotify"
)

func main() {
// Create a new watcher
watcher, err := fsnotify.NewWatcher()if err != nil {
log.Fatalf("Error creating watcher: %v", err)
}
defer watcher.Close()

// Start watching a directory
err = watcher.Add("./watched_directory")if err != nil {
log.Fatalf("Error adding directory to watcher: %v", err)
}
```

81

```go
// Start the event loopfor {
select {
case event, ok := <-watcher.Events:if !ok {
return
}
fmt.Printf("Event: %s\n", event)
if    event.Op&fsnotify.Write    ==    fsnotify.Write    {
fmt.Printf("Modified file: %s\n", event.Name)
}
if    event.Op&fsnotify.Create    ==    fsnotify.Create    {
fmt.Printf("Created file: %s\n", event.Name)
}
if    event.Op&fsnotify.Remove    ==    fsnotify.Remove    {
fmt.Printf("Deleted file: %s\n", event.Name)
}

case err, ok := <-watcher.Errors:if !ok {
return
}
log.Printf("Error: %v\n", err)
}
}
}
```

5.3.3 Running the Application

Create the directory you want to watch:
```shell
mkdir watched_directory
```

Run your application:
```shell
go run main.go
```

In another terminal, create, modify, or delete files in the `watched_directory` and observe how your application responds to various system events.

5.4 Handling User Input Events

Interactivity is key in many applications. For this purpose, we can utilize the `github.com/eiannone/keyboard` package to listen to keyboard events. ### 5.4.1 Installing the Keyboard Library
Use the following command to add the keyboard library to your project:

```shell
go get github.com/eiannone/keyboard
```

5.4.2 Listening for Keyboard Events

Now, we will enhance our previous example by adding keyboard event handling:

```go
package main

import ("fmt"
"log"                    "github.com/eiannone/keyboard"
```

```go
    "github.com/fsnotify/fsnotify"
)

func main() {
// Create a new watcher

watcher, err := fsnotify.NewWatcher()if err != nil {
log.Fatalf("Error creating watcher: %v", err)
}
defer watcher.Close()

// Start watching a directory
err = watcher.Add("./watched_directory")if err != nil {
log.Fatalf("Error adding directory to watcher: %v", err)
}

// Start listening for keyboard inputsgo func() {
if err := keyboard.Open(); err != nil { log.Fatalf("Error
opening keyboard: %v", err)
}
defer keyboard.Close()for {
char, key, err := keyboard.GetKey()if err != nil {
log.Fatalf("Error reading keyboard input: %v", err)
}
if key == keyboard.KeyEnter { fmt.Println("Enter key
pressed, exiting...")return
```

```
}
}()

}
fmt.Printf("You pressed: %s (key: %v)\n", string(char),
key)


// Start the event loopfor {
select {
case event, ok := <-watcher.Events:if !ok {
return
}
fmt.Printf("Event: %s\n", event)
// Handle file events as earlier...

case err, ok := <-watcher.Errors:if !ok {
return
}
log.Printf("Error: %v\n", err)
}
}
}
` ` `
```

5.5 Putting It All Together

With the above snippets, you can now create an application that listens for both file system changes and keyboard events simultaneously. This combination can serve as a foundation for more complex applicationsthat require multi-event handling, such as a real-time file monitoring system or a responsive user interface.

In this chapter, we explored the essentials of working with system events in GO, focusing on file system andkeyboard events. We covered setting up an environment, using third-party libraries like `fsnotify` and `keyboard`, and creating interactive applications that respond to system and user actions. As you continue your journey with GO, think about other types of events you may want to handle, such as network events or GUI interactions. The concepts laid out in this chapter form a solid basis for building responsive applications.

Monitoring System Events with Go

Go, with its efficient concurrency model, straightforward syntax, and powerful standard library, offers an excellent platform for building event monitoring solutions. This chapter explores how to leverage Go to monitor system events effectively, allowing you to detect anomalies, gather metrics, and respond to changesin real-time.

Understanding System Events

Before diving into the nitty-gritty of implementing monitoring systems, it's vital to understand what constitutes a system event. In the context of software and infrastructure, events can be anything from:

File changes: When a file is created, modified, or deleted.

Network activity: Incoming or outgoing data packets, connection requests.
Process state changes: Starting, stopping, and crashing of applications.
Resource utilization: CPU load, memory consumption, disk I/O.

Each of these events can provide insights into the overall health and performance of your applications and infrastructure.

Setting Up Your Go Environment

To get started with monitoring system events in Go, ensure that you have the Go programming environment properly set up:

Download and Install Go: Visit the official Go website (golang.org) and follow the installation instructions.
Create a New Project: Create a directory for your project. For example, `mkdir event-monitoring && cd event-monitoring`.
Initialize Go Modules: Use Go modules to manage your dependencies by running `go mod init event-monitoring`.

Key Libraries for Monitoring System Events

Go offers several libraries that can aid in system monitoring. Some notable ones include:

fsnotify: This is a cross-platform file system

notifications library that enables you to monitor file changes.
gopsutil: This library is particularly useful for gathering information about system usage (CPU, memory, disk, network).
Prometheus Go client: If you are interested in collecting metrics from your applications, this library allows you to expose those metrics in a format that Prometheus can scrape.

To install these libraries, you can run:

```bash
go get golang.org/x/sys
go get github.com/fsnotify/fsnotify go get github.com/shirou/gopsutil/cpu
go get github.com/shirou/gopsutil/mem
go get github.com/prometheus/client_golang/prometheus
```

Monitoring File Changes

One common scenario in monitoring is watching for changes in specific files or directories. The `fsnotify` library serves as an excellent tool for this purpose. Below is a simple example of how to monitor a directory for file changes:

```go
package main
```

```go
import (
"fmt"
"log" "github.com/fsnotify/fsnotify"
)

func main() {
watcher, err := fsnotify.NewWatcher()if err != nil {
log.Fatal(err)
}
defer watcher.Close()
done := make(chan bool)go func() {
for {
select {
case event, ok := <-watcher.Events:if !ok {
return
}
if    event.Op&fsnotify.Write    ==    fsnotify.Write    {
fmt.Printf("Modified file: %s\n", event.Name)
}
case err, ok := <-watcher.Errors:if !ok {
return




}
}
}()

}
log.Println("Error:", err)


err = watcher.Add("./monitored_directory")if err != nil {
```

```
        log.Fatal(err)



    }
    ```

}
<-done
```

In this code, we create a new file watcher that monitors a directory called `monitored_directory`. Whenever a file is modified, an event is triggered, and we log the change.

## Monitoring System Performance

Gathering performance metrics such as CPU and memory usage gives valuable insights into system health. With `gopsutil`, you can fetch this information easily. Here's how to achieve that:

```go
package main

import (
"fmt"
"time"                    "github.com/shirou/gopsutil/cpu"
"github.com/shirou/gopsutil/mem"
)

func main() {for {
cpuPercent, err := cpu.Percent(time.Second, false)if err !=
nil {
fmt.Println("Error getting CPU percent:", err)continue
```
```

```go
    }
  }
```

```go
    }
    v, _ := mem.VirtualMemory()
    fmt.Printf("CPU   Usage:   %.2f%%,   Memory   Usage:
    %.2f%%\n", cpuPercent[0], v.UsedPercent)time.Sleep(5 *
    time.Second)
```

This code snippet retrieves CPU and memory usage statistics every five seconds, allowing you to monitor system performance continuously.

Integrating with Prometheus

For a more advanced and scalable monitoring solution, consider integrating your application with Prometheus. This setup allows for metric scraping and visualization. Here's a simple example:

```go
package main

import (
"net/http"
"github.com/prometheus/client_golang/prometheus"
"github.com/prometheus/client_golang/prometheus/promhttp"
)

var (
```

```go
cpuUsage            =           prometheus.NewGaugeVec(
prometheus.GaugeOpts{
Name: "cpu_usage_percent", Help: "CPU usage
percentage",

},
[]string{"instance"},
)
)

func init() { prometheus.MustRegister(cpuUsage)
}

func recordMetrics() {go func() {
for {
// Simulate CPU usage metric recording
cpuUsage.WithLabelValues("localhost").Set(getCpuUsage
())time.Sleep(5 * time.Second)
}
}()
}

func getCpuUsage() float64 {
// Logic to retrieve CPU usage should be placed here (use
gopsutil or similar)return 50.0 // Placeholder value
}

func main() { recordMetrics()
http.Handle("/metrics",                 promhttp.Handler())
http.ListenAndServe(":8080", nil)
}
```
```
```

In this example, we set up a Prometheus endpoint for scraping metrics at `/metrics`. The `cpuUsage` metric simulates monitoring CPU usage periodically.

Monitoring system events with Go is both straightforward and powerful, allowing you to create bespoke solutions tailored to your specific needs. Whether you are monitoring file changes, tracking resource utilization, or integrating with scalable metric systems like Prometheus, Go provides the tools necessary to build effective monitoring solutions.

Event-Driven Programming in Go

Go, with its concurrency model, channels, and goroutines, provides a robust framework for implementing event-driven architectures.

In this chapter, we will explore the fundamentals of event-driven programming in Go, cover essential concepts, and present practical examples. Whether you are building a web application, a real-time messaging system, or an interactive user interface, understanding event-driven programming in Go will enhance your software design capabilities.

Core Concepts in Event-Driven Programming
Events and Event Handlers
At the heart of event-driven programming lies the concept of events. An event can be anything that happens in a program—such as a user clicking a button, receiving a message from a server, or detecting a change in a data

source. An event handler is a function or method that is invoked in response to an event.

In Go, we can define events as specific types and associate them with a set of handlers. This modularapproach allows for cleaner code and improved separation of concerns.

Event Loop

An event loop is a programming construct that waits for and dispatches events or messages in a program. In Go, we can achieve this using goroutines and channels. The event loop continuously listens for incoming events, processes them, and invokes the corresponding handlers.

Concurrency with Goroutines

Goroutines are lightweight, independently executing functions that can run concurrently with other functions. This feature of Go simplifies the implementation of event-driven systems since handlers can be executed asynchronously. By leveraging goroutines, we can respond to multiple events simultaneously without blocking the main execution thread.

Implementing an Event-Driven System in Go### Step 1: Defining an Event Type
Let's start by defining a simple event type and its associated data.

```go
package main
```

```go
import ("fmt"
"time"
)

// Event represents a custom event that carries a message.
type Event struct {
Message string
}
```

Step 2: Creating an Event Handler

Next, we create an event handler function that processes the event.

```go
// HandleEvent processes the incoming event. func
HandleEvent(event Event) {
fmt.Printf("Event received: %s\n", event.Message)
}
```

Step 3: Setting Up the Event Loop

Now, we set up an event loop using a channel to communicate events.

```go
func main() {
eventChannel := make(chan Event)

go func() {
// Simulating events being generatedfor i := 1; i <= 5; i++
```

```go
{
eventChannel <- Event{Message: fmt.Sprintf("Event %d",
i)}time.Sleep(1 * time.Second)
}
close(eventChannel) // Close the channel when done
}()

// Event loop
for event := range eventChannel {HandleEvent(event)
}
}
```

Explanation In the code above:
We define an `Event` struct to encapsulate the event data.
`HandleEvent` is a function that will be the event
handler, processing the data received.
An event loop is initiated using a goroutine that generates
events and sends them through a channel.
The main loop listens for events on the channel and calls
the appropriate handler. ### Step 4: Handling
Concurrency
To take full advantage of Go's concurrency features, we
can modify the event handler to run in a separate
goroutine. This allows for multiple events to be processed
simultaneously.

```go
func HandleEvent(event Event) {

go func() {
// Simulating a processing delay time.Sleep(2 *
time.Second)
```

```go
    fmt.Printf("Processed: %s\n", event.Message)
}()
}
```
```

Now, each event is handled in its own goroutine, allowing stronger parallelism in the event processing. ## Real-World Use Case: Building a Simple Web Server
Event-driven programming is prevalent in web server development, where various HTTP requests can trigger different actions. Let's see how to implement a simple HTTP server in Go using the principles of event-driven programming.

### Step 1: Setting Up the HTTP Server

We will create a simple web server that processes GET requests.

```go
package main

import ( "fmt" "net/http"
)

func main() {
http.HandleFunc("/", func(w http.ResponseWriter, r *http.Request) {
event := Event{Message: fmt.Sprintf("Received request: %s", r.URL.Path)} go HandleEvent(event) // Handle the event concurrently w.Write([]byte("Request received"))
})
```
```

```
fmt.Println("Server     is     running     on     :8080")
http.ListenAndServe(":8080", nil)
}
```

ExplanationIn this example:
We set up a basic HTTP server that listens for requests.
Upon receiving a request, we create an event and call `HandleEvent` in a separate goroutine, allowing the server to remain responsive to incoming requests.

Event-driven programming in Go offers a powerful model for managing asynchronous tasks and building responsive applications. Leveraging features such as goroutines and channels, developers can create efficient, scalable systems capable of handling numerous events concurrently. As you've seen in this chapter, understanding the principles of event-driven programming can significantly improve the design and functionality of your Go applications.

Chapter 6: Inter-Process Communication (IPC) with Pipes

In Go, one of the simplest and most effective methods for IPC is using pipes. Pipes provide a way for data to flow between processes in a unidirectional manner, forming the backbone of many concurrent programmingscenarios.

Understanding Pipes

A pipe is a data channel that can be used for communication between different processes. In the context of Go, pipes are often utilized for sending bytes from one process to another, allowing for efficient data transfer. Pipes can be either unnamed, where they exist only between the connected processes, or named, where they can be accessed by any process by name.

In Go, the `os/exec` package facilitates the creation of processes and the management of their IO, allowing developers to set up pipes easily.

Creating a Pipe

To demonstrate IPC with pipes in Go, let's start by creating a simple program where we will set up a pipe between the main process and a child process.

```go
package main
```

```go
import ("fmt"
"io"
"os" "os/exec"
)

func main() {
// Create a pipe
r, w, err := os.Pipe()if err != nil {
fmt.Println("Error creating pipe:", err)return
}

// Create a command that will read from the pipecmd :=
exec.Command("grep", "hello") cmd.Stdin = r

// Start the commanderr = cmd.Start()
if err != nil {
fmt.Println("Error starting command:", err)return
}

// Write to the pipe
_, err = w.Write([]byte("hello world\n"))if err != nil {
fmt.Println("Error writing to pipe:", err)return
}
_, err = w.Write([]byte("goodbye\n"))if err != nil {
fmt.Println("Error writing to pipe:", err)return
}

// Close the write end of the pipew.Close()

// Wait for the command to finisherr = cmd.Wait()
if err != nil {
fmt.Println("Error waiting for command:", err)return
}
```

```
fmt.Println("Command completed successfully.")
}
```

Explanation of the Code

Creating the Pipe: We use `os.Pipe()` to create a pipe, obtaining two file descriptors: one for reading (`r`) and one for writing (`w`).

Setting Up the Command: We create a command using `exec.Command` that reads from the pipe. In this example, we're using `grep` to filter input lines containing the word "hello".

Starting the Command: The command is started with `cmd.Start()`, and it is now waiting for input from the pipe.

Writing to the Pipe: We can write data to the pipe using the writer returned from `os.Pipe()`. The first string "hello world\n" will cause `grep` to output it, while "goodbye\n" will be ignored since it doesn't match.

Closing the Pipe: Closing the writer signifies that no more data will be sent, allowing the command to complete its execution.

Waiting for Completion: Finally, we use `cmd.Wait()` to wait for the command to finish running. ### Error Handling
Error handling is crucial when working with I/O

operations. In this example, we check for errors at each step of the process, from creating the pipe to writing to it, ensuring that the program can handle issues gracefully.

Using Buffered Pipes

In certain scenarios, an unbuffered pipe might lead to performance bottlenecks. Go provides a way to create buffered pipes by using `bytes.Buffer` or a `bufio.Writer`. These can help in managing larger volumes of data without blocking.

Pipes offer a straightforward and powerful means of achieving Inter-Process Communication in Go applications. Whether you're building command-line tools, server applications, or any system that requires running multiple processes, understanding how to implement and manage pipes is vital. In this chapter, we've covered the basic mechanics of creating and using pipes in Go, along with considerations for error handling and performance.

Using Pipes for IPC in Go

Inter-process communication (IPC) is a crucial aspect of modern software development, particularly when designing applications that require different parts to work together effectively. In Go, one powerful mechanism for IPC is the use of pipes. In this chapter, we will explore what pipes are, how they can be utilized in Go for IPC, and provide practical examples to solidify your understanding.

What Are Pipes?

102

Pipes are a method for different processes to communicate with one another, where the output of one process serves as the input to another. This communication can happen in two primary forms:

Unidirectional Pipes: Data flows in one direction - from the writer process to the reader process.
Bidirectional Pipes: Data can flow both ways, allowing two processes to exchange messages back and forth.

In Go, pipes are implemented using the `os.Pipe()` function, which creates a pair of linked file descriptors. One file descriptor is for reading, and the other is for writing. This allows one goroutine to write data to the pipe while another goroutine reads from it.

Creating a Pipe in Go

To engage with pipes in Go, we first need to create a pipe. The following example demonstrates how to set up a basic unidirectional pipe:

```go
package main

import ("fmt"
"io"
"os"
)

func main() {
// Create a pipe
```

```go
reader, writer, err := os.Pipe()if err != nil {
fmt.Println("Error creating pipe:", err)return
}

// Write to the pipe in a separate goroutinego func() {
defer writer.Close()
message := "Hello, IPC via pipes in Go!\n"
_, err := writer.Write([]byte(message))if err != nil {
fmt.Println("Error writing to pipe:", err)
}
}()

// Read from the pipe in the main goroutinebuffer :=
make([]byte, 128)
n, err := reader.Read(buffer)
if err != nil && err != io.EOF { fmt.Println("Error reading
from pipe:", err)
}

// Print the received messagefmt.Print(string(buffer[:n]))
}
```

Explanation of the Code

Creating the Pipe: We utilize `os.Pipe()` to create a pipe, which returns a `reader` and `writer`. The reader is used to read data from the pipe, while the writer sends data into it.

Writing to the Pipe: We launch a new goroutine where we write a message into the pipe using the writer. It is essential to close the writer after we're done sending data to signal that there is no more data to read.

Reading from the Pipe: In the main goroutine, we read data from the pipe into a buffer. The `Read` method will return the number of bytes read and an error if encountered. After reading, we print the message to the console.

Handling Errors

Error handling is vital in IPC applications. In the above code, we handle potential errors when creating the pipe, writing to the pipe, and reading from the pipe. This ensures that we can respond gracefully to any issues that may occur during communication.

Bidirectional Communication

While the above example demonstrates unidirectional communication, you may need to implement a bidirectional pipe. This can be accomplished by creating two separate pipes. Below is an example:

```go
package main

import ("fmt"
"io"
"os"
)

func main() {
// Create two pipes for bidirectional communication
```

```go
reader1, writer1, _ := os.Pipe()
reader2, writer2, _ := os.Pipe()

// Goroutine for writing message to the first pipe go func()
{
defer writer1.Close()

message    :=    "Message    from    Writer    1\n"
writer1.Write([]byte(message))
}()

// Goroutine for writing message to the second pipe go
func() {
defer writer2.Close()
message    :=    "Message    from    Writer    2\n"
writer2.Write([]byte(message))
}()

// Read from the first pipe buffer1 := make([]byte, 128)
n1,         _            :=            reader1.Read(buffer1)
fmt.Print(string(buffer1[:n1]))

// Read from the second pipe buffer2 := make([]byte, 128)
n2,         _            :=            reader2.Read(buffer2)
fmt.Print(string(buffer2[:n2]))
}
```

In this example, we create two pipes: one for each direction of communication. Each goroutine writes messages to its respective writer, and the main goroutine reads from both readers.

Pipes are a powerful IPC mechanism in Go that enables effective communication between different processes or goroutines. This chapter has provided an introduction to the concept of pipes, how to create them, and practical examples of unidirectional and bidirectional communication.

Advanced IPC Patterns in Go

With Go's concurrency model and rich set of primitives, IPC can be implemented elegantly and efficiently. In this chapter, we will delve into advanced IPC patterns in Go, exploring techniques like channels, goroutines, and third-party libraries that facilitate communication between processes.

Introduction to IPC in Go

Go's powerful concurrency features allow developers to create robust applications that can perform multiple tasks simultaneously. Go's goroutines, lightweight threads managed by the Go runtime, are designed to handle concurrent tasks efficiently. At the same time, channels serve as the primary means for goroutines to communicate with one another, allowing for both synchronization and data sharing.

While Go's native features are often sufficient for intra-process communication, situations may arise where IPC is required between separate processes. This chapter will explore advanced IPC patterns that leverage Go's capabilities, along with external tools and libraries.

1. IPC Fundamentals in Go

Before diving into advanced patterns, it's important to grasp the basic concepts of IPC: ### 1.1. Channels
Channels in Go are used to pass data between goroutines. The primary types of channels include:

Unbuffered Channels: These are blocking channels; the sending goroutine waits until the receiving goroutine reads the data.

Buffered Channels: These allow a limited number of values to be sent without immediately being received. If the buffer is full, the sending goroutine blocks until space is available.

1.2. Goroutines

Goroutines are lightweight, allowing for concurrent execution of functions. They are simple to use:

```go
go func() {
// Code to execute in a new goroutine
}()
```

2. Advanced IPC Patterns ### 2.1. Worker Pools
One common pattern for managing concurrent tasks is the worker pool. In this approach, a fixed number of workers (goroutines) process jobs from a shared channel. This pattern effectively regulates resource usage and

maximizes throughput while ensuring that no single resource is overwhelmed.

```go
type Job struct {Id int

// additional job data...
}

func worker(jobs <-chan Job) {for job := range jobs {
// Process job
}
}

func main() {
jobs := make(chan Job, 100)

for w := 1; w <= 5; w++ {go worker(jobs)
}

for j := 1; j <= 10; j++ {jobs <- Job{Id: j}
}

close(jobs)
}
```

2.2. Publish-Subscribe (Pub/Sub)

The Pub/Sub pattern is useful in scenarios where multiple components need to react to events. In Go, you can implement this pattern using channels and goroutines, allowing subscribers to receive notifications when an event occurs.

```go
type Event struct {Message string
}

type Publisher struct {
subscribers map[chan Event]struct{}
}

func (p *Publisher) Subscribe() chan Event { ch :=
make(chan Event)
p.subscribers[ch] = struct{}{}return ch
}

func (p *Publisher) Publish(event Event) {for ch := range
p.subscribers {
ch <- event
}
}
```

2.3. Message Queues with Redis

While Go's channels are powerful within a single application, they are not suitable for communication between separate processes. For cross-process communication, integrating a message broker like Redis can facilitate messaging between disparate components. Using the `go-redis` package, we can easily implement a message queue.

```go
```

```go
import "github.com/go-redis/redis/v8"

func publishMessage(ctx context.Context, rdb *redis.Client, message string) { rdb.Publish(ctx, "my_channel", message)
}

func subscribeToMessages(ctx context.Context, rdb *redis.Client) { pubsub := rdb.Subscribe(ctx, "my_channel")
ch := pubsub.Channel()

for msg := range ch { fmt.Println(msg.Payload)
}
}
```

2.4. gRPC for Remote Procedure Calls

gRPC is a high-performance RPC framework that utilizes HTTP/2 for transport. It's an excellent choice for building microservices in Go, where services need to communicate with each other. With Protocol Buffers for serialization, gRPC allows for type-safe messages across the wire.

```go
// Define service in .proto file

service UserService {
rpc GetUser(UserRequest) returns (UserResponse);
}

// Implementing the servicetype server struct {
```

```
pb.UnimplementedUserServiceServer
}

func (s *server) GetUser(ctx context.Context, req
*pb.UserRequest) (*pb.UserResponse, error) {
// Fetch and return user data
}
```

3. Considerations for IPC

When designing IPC solutions, consider the trade-offs of the methods used. Key factors include:

Latency: Some methods introduce overhead (like network delays in message queues).
Complexity: External systems like Redis add complexity that should be justified.
Scalability: Choose patterns that easily scale as your application grows.

In this chapter, we explored advanced IPC patterns in Go that make the most of its concurrency model while also accommodating external systems. We covered worker pools, Pub/Sub systems, message queues using Redis, and gRPC for inter-service communication. Properly understanding and implementing these patterns can greatly enhance your ability to manage complex applications effectively. As always, the right IPC solution will depend on the specific requirements and architecture of your system.

Chapter 7: Automating Hardware with Go

In this chapter, we will explore how to automate hardware tasks using the Go programming language and the libraries that can help streamline this process.

7.1 Introduction to Hardware Automation

Hardware automation refers to the techniques and tools used to control physical devices automatically without human intervention. These devices can range from simple sensors and actuators to complex robotic systems. Go's concurrency model makes it a suitable choice for handling multiple hardware components simultaneously, allowing developers to focus on creating efficient and maintainable systems.

7.2 Setting Up Go for Hardware Automation

Before diving into hardware automation, we need to set up our Go environment. You should have Go installed on your machine. To check if Go is installed, you can use the following command:

```bash
go version
```

If Go is not installed, you can download it from the official [Go website](https://golang.org/dl/). Once Go is set up, we will also need access to libraries that facilitate hardware interaction, such as `periph.io` for interfacing with GPIO pins, I2C, SPI, and other protocols commonly used in hardware development.

Installing Necessary Libraries

To install the `periph.io` library, you can run:

```bash
go get periph.io/x/periph
```

This library provides a comprehensive API for interacting with hardware components and devices. ## 7.3 GPIO Control with Go
One of the most common tasks in hardware automation is controlling General Purpose Input/Output (GPIO) pins. These pins are utilized for various input and output operations, such as reading sensor data or controlling LEDs. Below is an example of how to set up a GPIO pin as an output and control an LED.

Example: Blinking an LED

```go
package main

import (
    "periph.io/x/periph/io/gpio"
    "periph.io/x/periph/host"
    "time"
)

func main() {
    // Initialize periph.io
```

```go
if _, err := host.Init(); err != nil {panic(err)
}

// Get the LED pin (e.g., GPIO17)
led := gpio.MustNewPin("GPIO17", gpio.Out)

// Blink the LEDfor {
led.Out(gpio.High) // Turn the LED on time.Sleep(500 *
time.Millisecond) led.Out(gpio.Low) // Turn the LED off
time.Sleep(500 * time.Millisecond)
}
}
```

In this example, we initialize the periph library, select a GPIO pin, and toggle the state of the LED between on and off states every half a second. The simplicity of code illustrates how Go makes hardware control intuitive.

7.4 Reading Sensor Data

One of the many applications of hardware automation is collecting data from sensors. For this section, wewill read temperature data from a hypothetical temperature sensor connected via I2C.

Example: Reading Temperature from a Sensor

```go
package main

import ("fmt"
"periph.io/x/periph/conn/i2c" "periph.io/x/periph/host"
```

```go
"periph.io/x/periph/devices/dht"
)

func main() {
// Initialize the periph library
if _, err := host.Init(); err != nil {panic(err)
}

// Establish I2C connection (hypothetical) bus, err :=
i2c.New("I2C0")
if err != nil {panic(err)
}
sensor := dht.New(bus, 0x76) // Example address for a
DHT sensor

// Read temperature and humidityfor {
temp, humidity, err := sensor.Read()if err != nil {
fmt.Println("Failed to read sensor:", err)continue
}
fmt.Printf("Temperature: %.2f°C, Humidity: %.2f%%\n",
temp, humidity)
<-time.After(2 * time.Second) // Delay between readings
}
}
```
```

This code initializes an I2C bus and a DHT sensor, reading
the temperature and humidity data every two seconds.
The `periph` library abstracts the complexity of
communication, allowing developers to focus on
application logic.

## 7.5 Automating Tasks with Goroutines
```

Another significant advantage of using Go for hardware automation is the ease of handling concurrent executions. Goroutines, which are lightweight threads managed by the Go runtime, can be used to run multiple tasks simultaneously, making it simpler to monitor sensors or control multiple devices without blocking the main thread.

Example: Concurrent Sensor Readings

Imagine we want to read data from multiple sensors. By leveraging goroutines, we can handle this efficiently. The following example demonstrates how to read temperature from multiple sensors at once.

```go
package main

import ("fmt"
"sync"
"time"                    "periph.io/x/periph/devices/dht"
"periph.io/x/periph/host"
)

func        readTemperature(sensor        *dht.Dev,      wg
*sync.WaitGroup)    {    defer   wg.Done()  //   Indicate
completion

temp, humidity, err := sensor.Read()if err != nil {
fmt.Println("Failed to read sensor:", err)return
}
fmt.Printf("Sensor   ID   %d  -  Temperature:   %.2f°C,
Humidity: %.2f%%\n", sensor.ID, temp, humidity)
```

```go
}

func main() {
if _, err := host.Init(); err != nil {panic(err)

}

// Create    wait    group    for    goroutines    var    wg
sync.WaitGroup

// Assuming we have multiple sensors
sensors  :=  []*dht.Dev{device1,  device2,  device3}  //
Hypothetical devices

for _, sensor := range sensors {wg.Add(1)
go readTemperature(sensor, &wg) // Launch goroutine
for each sensor
}

wg.Wait() // Wait for all goroutines to finish
}
```
` ` `

In this snippet, we launch a goroutine for each sensor,
allowing them to read data concurrently. The use of
`sync.WaitGroup` ensures that the main function waits
until all sensor readings complete. This model can easily
scale to handle many devices.

In this chapter, we explored the fundamental concepts of
hardware automation using the Go programming
language. From GPIO control to reading sensor data and
leveraging goroutines for concurrency, Go provides a

powerful and accessible way to automate tasks involving hardware.

As we strive for smarter systems in the context of IoT and related domains, the ability to automate hardware effectively will remain a vital skill for developers. With tools like `periph.io`, Go bridges the gap between software and hardware, allowing for thrilling innovations and applications.

Managing USB Devices with Go

In today's interconnected world, USB devices are omnipresent. From keyboards and mice to storage devices and cameras, they serve countless functions across a wide range of applications.

1. Understanding USB Basics

Before we dive into managing USB devices with Go, let's briefly cover some fundamental concepts about USB (Universal Serial Bus):

USB Types: There are several types of USB connectors, including USB-A, USB-B, USB-C, and mini/micro variants.
USB Classes: USB devices are categorized into various classes (like mass storage, audio, video, etc.). Each class has a specific protocol and controls.
Device Drivers: Each USB device requires a corresponding driver for communication with the host system. Some USB devices are plug-and-play, while others

may require manual driver installation.

2. Setting Up the Go Environment

To get started, you need to have Go installed on your computer. You can download it from the [official Go website](https://golang.org/dl/). Optionally, it's also beneficial to have basic knowledge of Go's syntax and structure.

Installation of Dependencies

To manage USB devices in Go, we will leverage existing libraries such as `libusb`, which provides an interface for USB device manipulation. On Linux or macOS, you can use the Go wrapper for `libusb`, called `github.com/usb-serial-for-android/usb-serial-for-android`. You can install it with the command:
```bash
go get github.com/usb-serial-for-android/usb-serial-for-android
```

3. Accessing USB Devices

Let's create a simple Go program to list the USB devices connected to a system.

```go
package main

import ("fmt"
"github.com/usb-serial-for-android/usb-serial-for-
```

```go
    android""log"
)

func main() {
ctx, err := usb.NewContext()if err != nil {

log.Fatalf("Error initializing USB context: %v", err)
}
defer ctx.Close()

devices, err := ctx.ListDevices()if err != nil {
log.Fatalf("Error listing devices: %v", err)
}

for _, dev := range devices {
fmt.Printf("Device Name: %s, Vendor ID: 0x%04x,
Product ID: 0x%04x\n", dev.Name(), dev.VendorID(),
dev.ProductID())
}
}
```
```

### Explanation of the Code

**Initialization of USB Context:** A USB context is
created to manage the interaction with USBsubsystem.
**Listing Devices:** The `ListDevices()` method retrieves
a list of USB devices connected to the system.
**Looping Through Devices:** Each device's name,
vendor ID, and product ID are printed to the console.##
4. Communicating with USB Devices
Once we have access to USB devices, the next step is to
establish communication. The following example
```

demonstrates how to open a USB device and send data to it.

Example: Sending Data to a USB Device

```go
package main

import ("fmt"
"github.com/usb-serial-for-android/usb-serial-for-android""log"
)

func main() {
ctx, err := usb.NewContext()if err != nil {
log.Fatalf("Error initializing USB context: %v", err)
}
defer ctx.Close()

devices, err := ctx.ListDevices()if err != nil {
log.Fatalf("Error listing devices: %v", err)
}

if len(devices) == 0 {
log.Fatal("No USB devices found")
}

// Selecting the first devicedevice := devices[0]
err = device.Open()if err != nil {
log.Fatalf("Error opening device: %v", err)
}
defer device.Close()
```

```go
data := []byte("Hello USB Device")
_, err = device.Write(data)if err != nil {
log.Fatalf("Error writing data to device: %v", err)
}

fmt.Println("Data sent to USB device successfully!")
}
```

Explanation of the Code

Open Device: We open the desired USB device for communication.
Write Data: The `Write()` method sends a byte slice to the device.
Handle Errors: Ensure proper error handling throughout the process. ## 5. Handling Data from USB Devices
Interacting with USB devices doesn't only involve sending data. Often, we need to read data from these devices as well. Let's examine how to achieve this:

Example: Reading Data from a USB Device

```go
package main

import ("fmt"
"github.com/usb-serial-for-android/usb-serial-for-android""log"
)

func main() {
```

```go
ctx, err := usb.NewContext()if err != nil {
log.Fatalf("Error initializing USB context: %v", err)
}
defer ctx.Close()

devices, err := ctx.ListDevices()if err != nil {
log.Fatalf("Error listing devices: %v", err)
}

if len(devices) == 0 {
log.Fatal("No USB devices found")

}

// Selecting the first devicedevice := devices[0]
err = device.Open()if err != nil {
log.Fatalf("Error opening device: %v", err)
}
defer device.Close()

buffer := make([]byte, 64) // Create a buffer for reading
datan, err := device.Read(buffer)
if err != nil {
log.Fatalf("Error reading data from device: %v", err)
}

fmt.Printf("Received data: %s\n", string(buffer[:n]))
}
```
```

### Explanation of the Code

**Read Data:** We declare a buffer to store the incoming

124
```

data from the USB device.
Print Received Data: Upon successful reading, we convert the byte slice to a string and print the result.

With this foundational knowledge, you can start building applications that leverage USB device interactions for various use cases, whether they involve custom peripherals, data acquisition systems, or just enhancing usability by connecting diverse hardware. As you move forward, experiment with different USB device classes and explore the full capabilities that Go offers for USB management.

Handling Bluetooth Devices for Automation in GO

Bluetooth technology plays a crucial role in enabling seamless communication between devices without the need for a physical connection. This chapter will focus on handling Bluetooth devices using the Go programming language, facilitating the development of automation systems that can interact with various Bluetooth-enabled devices.

Understanding Bluetooth Technology

Before diving into how to manage Bluetooth devices with Go, it is essential to understand the fundamentals of Bluetooth technology. Bluetooth is a wireless communication standard that allows devices to exchange data over short distances. It operates within the 2.4 GHz frequency band and provides a reliable and energy-efficient method for communication.

Key Bluetooth Concepts

Bluetooth Profiles: These are standardized protocols that allow devices to communicate in specific contexts, such as audio streaming (A2DP), file transfer (FTP), and more.
Pairing: This is the process that allows Bluetooth devices to establish a trusted connection.
Services and Characteristics: In Bluetooth Low Energy (BLE), devices expose services that contain specific characteristics. These characteristics hold data that can be read or written.

Setting Up Your Go Environment

To handle Bluetooth devices in Go, you'll need to set up your development environment properly. Make sure you have:

Go installed: Download the latest version from the [official Go website](https://golang.org/dl/).
A compatible Bluetooth library: For Bluetooth operations in Go, the `tinygo/bluetooth` library is a great choice. It provides a robust API for scanning, connecting, and interacting with Bluetooth devices.

Installing the Bluetooth Library

You can install the Bluetooth library by running:

```bash
```

```
go get github.com/tinygo/bluetooth
```

Scanning for Bluetooth Devices

The first step in handling Bluetooth devices is to scan for available devices in the vicinity. Below is an example of how to perform a Bluetooth scan using the `tinygo/bluetooth` library.

```go
package main

import (
"fmt"
"log"
"time"

"tinygo/bluetooth"
)

func main() {
adapter := bluetooth.DefaultAdapter

if err := adapter.Enable(); err != nil {log.Fatal(err)
}

fmt.Println("Scanning for devices...")
adapter.Scan(func(adapter *bluetooth.Adapter, device bluetooth.DeviceInfo) { fmt.Printf("Found device: %s - %s\n", device.Address.String(), device.Name())
})
```

```
}
```

```
// Scan for a limited duration time.Sleep(10 *
time.Second) adapter.StopScan() fmt.Println("Scan
finished.")
```

Explanation

Enable Adapter: The first step is to enable the default
Bluetooth adapter.
Scanning for Devices: The `Scan` function initiates a
scanning process that will invoke a callback function each
time a device is found.
10-Second Scan: The program scans for 10 seconds
and then stops the scan.## Establishing a Connection
Once you have identified a Bluetooth device of interest,
the next step is to establish a connection. Below is an
example demonstrating how to connect to a device:

```go
package main

import (
"fmt"
"log"
"time"

"tinygo/bluetooth"
)
```

```go
func connectToDevice(address bluetooth.Address) {
adapter := bluetooth.DefaultAdapter

if err := adapter.Connect(address); err != nil {
log.Fatalf("Failed to connect: %s", err)
}
fmt.Printf("Connected to device: %s\n", address.String())
}

func main() {
// Assume we've found a device with this address
deviceAddress := bluetooth.Address{0x12, 0x34, 0x56, 0x78, 0x9A, 0xBC}connectToDevice(deviceAddress)

// This is where you would handle interaction with the device.time.Sleep(2 * time.Second)

adapter.Disconnect(deviceAddress)
fmt.Printf("Disconnected from device: %s\n", deviceAddress.String())
}
```
` ` `

Explanation

Connecting: We attempt to connect to a Bluetooth device using its address.
Disconnecting: After performing the intended operations (not shown for brevity), we disconnect fromthe device.

Communicating with Bluetooth Devices

Once connected, you can communicate with the Bluetooth device by reading and writing characteristics. This interaction varies according to the specific Bluetooth profile in use.

Reading Characteristics

Here's how to read a characteristic from a connected device:

```go
package main

import (
"fmt"
"log"

"tinygo/bluetooth"
)

func readCharacteristic(device bluetooth.DeviceInfo,
characteristic bluetooth.UUID) {
// Assuming we've already connected to the device var
value []byte

err := device.ReadCharacteristic(characteristic, &value)if
err != nil {
log.Fatalf("Failed to read characteristic: %s", err)
}

fmt.Printf("Characteristic Value: %v\n", value)
}
```

```go
func main() {
// Assume we have a connected device instance here var
connectedDevice bluetooth.DeviceInfo
// Example characteristic UUID (this should be replaced
by an actual UUID)


}
```
` ` `

charUUID := bluetooth.NewUUID16(0x2A00)
readCharacteristic(connectedDevice, charUUID)

Explanation

Reading the Characteristic: This function reads the value from a specific characteristic and prints it.
Characteristic UUID: Each characteristic has a unique identifier (UUID), which is essential for the communication.

Scanning for devices, establishing connections, and communicating with them are simplified through the structured API provided by the library. As you dive deeper into Bluetooth programming in Go, consider exploring additional features such as handling BLE notifications, working with multiple devices, and implementing automated tasks based on Bluetooth interactions.

Chapter 8: Memory Management in Go

In Go, an open-source programming language designed for simplicity and efficiency, memory management harnesses a variety of techniques to provide a robust environment for developers. This chapter explores the mechanisms of memory management in Go, focusing on its garbage collection, memory allocation strategies, and best practices for effective memory use.

8.1 Understanding Memory Management

Memory management refers to the process of controlling and coordinating computer memory, allocating portions of memory to various programs and reclaiming it when it is no longer needed. Proper memory management ensures that applications run smoothly, utilize memory effectively, and do not leak resources that can lead to performance degradation or crashes.

Go was designed with memory management in mind, emphasizing ease of use and efficiency. Go abstracts away many of the complexities associated with manual memory management, while still providing developers with the tools necessary to write high-performance applications.

8.2 Garbage Collection in Go

One of the standout features of Go's memory management system is its garbage collector (GC). Garbage collection in Go is automatic, meaning that programmers do not need to manually free memory. The GC periodically scans the memory heap to identify and reclaim memory that is no longer in use, thereby preventing memory leaks.

8.2.1 How Garbage Collection Works

Go employs a concurrent garbage collector that minimizes pause times, allowing applications to remain responsive even while garbage collection occurs. The garbage collector operates by utilizing a combination of the following strategies:

Mark and Sweep Algorithm: Go primarily uses a mark-and-sweep algorithm. The collector marks objects that are reachable from root pointers (such as stack variables and global variables). Once marking is completed, the collector sweeps through the heap and reclaims memory allocated to unmarked objects.

Generational GC: While Go does not adhere strictly to generational garbage collection, it utilizes certain aspects of this approach. Newly allocated memory is more likely to become unreachable quickly compared to long-lived objects, so the GC is optimized for handling short-lived objects efficiently.

Concurrent Execution: Go's garbage collector runs concurrently with the application, minimizing the disruption caused by collection activities. This means that while memory is being collected, the program continues executing, reducing latency and pause times.

8.2.2 Tuning the Garbage Collector

While Go's garbage collector is designed to work

intelligently out of the box, developers can tune certain parameters to optimize performance for specific applications. The `GOGC` environment variable controls the garbage collection frequency, adjusting the ratio of heap growth to trigger garbage collection cycles. Understanding and adjusting this parameter can help manage memory usage patterns in resource-intensive applications.

8.3 Memory Allocation Strategies

Go utilizes several strategies for memory allocation, which help it maintain efficiency and performance during runtime. Understanding these strategies is crucial for developers looking to optimize their applications.

8.3.1 Stack vs. Heap Allocation

In Go, variables can be allocated on the stack or the heap:

Stack Allocation: Local variables are typically allocated on the stack. The allocation and deallocation are fast and managed automatically when a function call is completed. The stack has a limited size, which can lead to a stack overflow if excessive memory is allocated.

Heap Allocation: When data needs to persist beyond the function call where it was created or is too large for the stack, it is allocated on the heap. Although heap allocation is slower than stack allocation, Go's efficient garbage collection mitigates potential downsides.

8.3.2 The `new` and `make` Functions

134

Go provides two built-in functions for memory allocation:

`new(Type)`: This function allocates zeroed storage for a new item of the specified type and returns a pointer to it. It is used primarily for allocating a pointer to a data structure.

`make(Type, ...) Type`: This function is specifically used for allocating and initializing slices, maps, and channels. `make` performs additional setup, such as creating an internal data structure or setting an initial size for slices.

8.3.3 Object Alignment and Caching

Go also takes into account memory alignment and caching. Aligned memory improves access speed due to how modern CPUs handle memory. Go aligns objects in memory to ensure that they fit efficiently within the CPU's cache lines. In doing so, the language seeks to minimize cache misses and optimize overall application performance.

8.4 Best Practices for Memory Management in Go

To make the most of Go's memory management capabilities, developers should consider the following best practices:

Minimize Object Creation: Reusing objects wherever possible can help reduce pressure on the garbage collector and improve performance. Consider using object pooling for frequently used objects.

Monitor Memory Usage: Utilize Go's profiling tools, such as `pprof`, to monitor memory allocation and usage patterns. Identifying memory-intensive functions can help optimize memory consumption.

Avoid Global Variables: While global variables may seem convenient, they can lead to unintended memory retention and complicate garbage collection. Instead, structure programs to pass data as function parameters.

Be Mindful of Slices and Maps: These data structures can lead to excessive memory allocation if not handled carefully. Understanding their internals can help mitigate unnecessary allocations.

Understand Lifetime and Scope: Being aware of variable lifetimes and scopes can help you make better decisions regarding memory usage and allocation.

Memory management in Go is designed to provide developers with a powerful, efficient, and user-friendly environment for building applications. By leveraging automatic garbage collection, optimized allocation strategies, and best practices, developers can focus on writing high-quality code without being bogged down by the complexities of manual memory management. As we continue to explore Go's features, understanding memory management becomes essential for leveraging the full potential of this innovative language.

Understanding Go's Garbage Collection

One of its standout features is its built-in garbage collection (GC) mechanism, which helps manage memory automatically. Understanding Go's garbage collection is crucial for developers who want to write efficient, high-performance applications. This chapter explores the principles behind Go's garbage collection, how it works, and best practices for leveraging GC in your Go applications.

1. The Need for Garbage Collection

In manual memory management systems, developers allocate and deallocate memory explicitly. This approach can lead to memory leaks when memory is not freed correctly, and dangling pointers, which reference memory that has already been freed. Garbage collection addresses these issues by automatically reclaiming memory that is no longer in use. In a language like Go, this allows developers to focus on application logic rather than memory handling.

2. How Go's Garbage Collector Works

Go's garbage collector employs a combination of techniques, primarily tracing garbage collection. The GC identifies which objects in memory are still accessible by the program, and those that are not are considered garbage and can be reclaimed.

2.1 Root Set

The garbage collection process begins by identifying the "root set." The root set includes global variables, stack variables, and other references that are directly accessible. Go's GC uses this root set to traverse the heap and determine which objects are reachable and which are not.

2.2 Mark and Sweep

Go's garbage collection algorithm primarily follows a **mark and sweep** approach:

Mark Phase: During this phase, the GC traverses the root set and recursively marks all reachable objects. Any object that can be accessed by following references from the root set is marked as "live."

Sweep Phase: After the marking phase, the GC scans the heap and reclaims memory from objects that were not marked. These objects are considered garbage because they are no longer accessible by any references in the program.

2.3 Generational GC

While Go's garbage collector does not traditionally implement a generational approach, recent improvements have incorporated aspects of this concept. Generational GC optimizes performance by exploiting the observation that most objects have relatively short lifespans. By handling young and old objects differently, it can reduce the frequency and duration of garbage collection pauses.

3. Concurrent Garbage Collection

One of the most significant strengths of Go's garbage collection is its concurrent nature. Unlike some traditional garbage collectors that stop the entire program during collection (known as stop-the-world pauses), Go's GC runs concurrently with the application on multiple goroutines.

3.1 Pause Time

Garbage collection pauses are typically short in Go, often measured in milliseconds. Developers can manage and minimize these pauses using techniques such as:

Reducing Allocation Rates: Frequent allocations can increase the overhead of garbage collection. By reusing objects and minimizing short-lived allocations, developers can reduce GC pressure.

Control of GC Throughput: Go allows developers to tune garbage collection settings through environment variables. The `GOGC` variable can be adjusted to set the garbage collection target percentage. Increasing `GOGC` reduces the frequency of collections by allowing the heap to grow larger before initiating GC.

4. Profiling and Debugging

To effectively manage memory and optimize garbage collection in Go applications, developers should utilize Go's profiling tools. The `pprof` package provides insights into memory allocation, including GC behavior.

4.1 Memory Profiling

Memory profiling can help identify memory usage patterns and potential memory leaks. Developers can analyze heap profiles to see the allocation of objects over time, understand which objects are consuming memory, and how the GC is performing.

4.2 Monitoring GC Performance

Using Go's built-in metrics, developers can monitor GC pause times and collect information on the frequency of garbage collection operations. This feedback is vital for understanding the performance implications of memory usage within an application.

5. Best Practices for Managing Memory in Go

While Go's garbage collection simplifies memory management, following best practices is still essential for optimal performance:

Limit Allocations: Minimize the number of allocations by using object pooling or reusing objects wherever possible. This reduces the workload on the garbage collector.

Use Value Types When Appropriate: For small data structures, consider using value types (structs) instead of pointer types. This can lead to fewer allocations and less pressure on the garbage collector.

Avoid Global State: Excessive reliance on global state can lead to complex references and increased GC workload. Encapsulate state within your components.

Use the `sync.Pool`: The `sync.Pool` type can be used for caching objects that are expensive to allocate, reducing the number of allocations and thus the load on the GC.

Be Mindful of Slice and Map Growth: Slices and maps can trigger more allocations when they grow. Understanding the internal mechanics of these structures can help manage memory more effectively.

Go's garbage collector is a powerful feature that alleviates the complexities of memory management, allowing developers to create efficient programs without focusing excessively on memory allocation and deallocation.

Optimizing Memory Usage in Go Applications

In Go, a language designed for simplicity and efficiency, understanding how to manage and optimize memory can lead to significant performance improvements, reduced latency, and lower resource consumption. This chapter delves into key techniques and best practices for optimizing memory usage in Go applications.

1. Understanding Memory Management in Go

Go has a built-in garbage collector that automatically manages memory allocation and deallocation. While this simplifies development and helps prevent memory leaks, it also introduces some overhead. To effectively optimize memory usage, it's crucial to know how Go's memory management works:

Heap and Stack Memory: Go divides memory into two segments—heap and stack. Stack memory is used for static memory allocation, where the size is known at compile time. In contrast, heap memory is used for dynamic memory allocation, where the size is determined at runtime, making it more flexible but also potentially more expensive in terms of allocation and garbage collection.

Garbage Collection: Go uses a concurrent garbage collector that automatically identifies and frees memory that is no longer in use. However, frequent allocations and deallocations can lead to higher levels of garbage collection activity, impacting performance. Understanding how and when the garbage collector runs can help in structuring your application to minimize its impact.

2. Techniques for Optimizing Memory Usage ### 2.1 Use Value Types When Possible
In Go, both value types (structs, arrays) and reference types (slices, maps, channels) can be used to store data. Value types are often more memory-efficient as they are allocated on the stack, reducing the overhead associated with heap memory management. In situations where copies of data are minimal and the data structures remain small, using value types can yield better performance.

2.2 Efficient Use of Slices and Arrays

Slices in Go are backed by arrays but have additional

142

overhead due to their metadata. Whenever possible, use arrays for fixed-size data as they are allocated directly on the stack. If you need the flexibility of a slice, consider conducting operations in batches to minimize slice overhead and reducing the number of allocations.

2.3 Pooling Objects with sync.Pool

One effective way to manage memory in Go applications is through object pooling using `sync.Pool`. This allows you to reuse previously allocated objects rather than allocating new objects every time, which can reduce memory fragmentation and garbage collection pressure. For example, if your application frequently creates temporary objects, using a pool can lead to significant performance improvements.

```go
package main

import (
"fmt"

"sync"
)

var workerPool = sync.Pool{New: func() interface{} {
return new(Worker) // Assuming Worker is a struct
},
}

func main() {
worker := workerPool.Get().(*Worker) // Get a Worker
```

143

from the pool
defer workerPool.Put(worker)   // Return it back to the
pool when done

// Use the worker...
}
```

### 2.4 Minimize Goroutines

While goroutines are lightweight, each goroutine allocates a small amount of memory for its stack. Hordes of goroutines can lead to significant memory use. To optimize, avoid launching too many goroutines simultaneously, and consider using worker pools to manage concurrent tasks more efficiently.

### 2.5 Beware of Memory Leaks

Even with garbage collection, memory leaks can still occur if you maintain references to objects that are no longer necessary. To prevent leaks, ensure that you do not unintentionally hold references to data structures that should be collected. Regular profiling and memory analysis using tools like `pprof` can help identify potential leaks in your application.

```shell
go tool pprof yourapp yourapp.prof
```

3. Profiling Memory Usage
```

To effectively optimize memory usage, you need to measure it. Go provides excellent profiling tools to help you analyze memory allocation patterns in your application:

pprof: The `net/http/pprof` package provides a convenient way to gather profiling information. By integrating it into your application, you can capture and analyze memory usage during runtime, helping identify bottlenecks and opportunities for optimization.

Heap Profiling: By enabling heap profiling, you can analyze which parts of your application consume the most memory. This profiling data can guide your optimization efforts, highlighting areas where you can reduce memory usage or refactor code.

4. Best Practices for Memory Optimization### 4.1 Use the Right Data Structures
Choosing the right data structure is crucial for optimal memory usage. Evaluate trade-offs between different data structures (e.g., maps vs. slices) considering factors such as access speed, memory overhead, and use case.

4.2 Avoid Unnecessary Allocations

Be mindful of unnecessary memory allocations, particularly in tight loops. Reuse existing structures whenever possible, and avoid allocating buffers that are not needed.

4.3 Monitor Memory Consumption

In production environments, continuously monitor memory consumption to catch issues as they arise. Tools like Prometheus and Grafana can help visualize memory use and alert you to potential issues.

4.4 Educate Your Team

Ensure your development team understands memory optimization principles and how to use Go's built-in tools effectively. Foster a culture of performance awareness to detect and address memory-related issues early in the development process.

Optimizing memory usage in Go applications requires a combination of understanding Go's memory management model, utilizing effective memory optimization techniques, and regularly profiling memory usage.

Chapter 9: Distributing Your Go Applications

Distributing your Go application effectively is crucial for getting it into the hands of users and ensuring its success. This chapter will guide you through the various strategies and tools available to package and share your Go applications with the world, from static binaries to containerized solutions.

1. Understanding Go's Compilation Model

Before diving into distribution options, it's essential to understand how Go compiles applications. Go is known for its ability to produce statically linked binaries. This means that when you compile your Go application, the resulting executable contains all the necessary dependencies bundled together.

Benefits:
Portability: Since the application is self-contained, it can run on any machine with the same architecture (e.g., Windows, Linux, macOS) without requiring users to install additional libraries or dependencies.
Simplicity: End users can execute your application easily, as all they need is to download the binary and run it.

Compiling for Different Architectures
One of the significant features of Go is cross-compilation. This allows you to build binaries for different architectures and operating systems from your

development machine. For example, you can compile a Linux executable on a macOS machine by setting the `GOOS` and `GOARCH` environment variables:

```bash
# For Linux
GOOS=linux GOARCH=amd64 go build -o myapp-linux-amd64

# For Windows
GOOS=windows GOARCH=amd64 go build -o myapp-windows-amd64.exe

# For macOS
GOOS=darwin GOARCH=amd64 go build -o myapp-darwin-amd64
```

2. Creating a Release Package

Once your application is compiled, the next step is to package it for distribution. A simple release package can include the following elements:

The compiled binary for each target platform.
A README file with installation instructions and usage information.
Configuration files, if applicable.
License files, if your application is open-source.

Tools for Creating Release Packages
Several tools can help automate the creation of release packages:

GoReleaser: GoReleaser is a powerful tool designed to make the process of releasing Go applicationsas simple as possible. It automates the packaging, auto-detects Git tags, generates changelogs, and can even publish your binaries to GitHub or other platforms.

```yaml
# Example .goreleaser.yml configurationbuild:
binaries:
name: myappgoos:
linux
darwin
windowsgoarch:
amd64
arm64
```

GitHub Releases: If you host your project on GitHub, you can take advantage of its release features tocreate a new release and upload your binaries easily. This allows users to download the version that matches their environment effortlessly.

3. Using Docker for Distribution

With the rise of containerization, distribution through Docker has become a popular option. Docker allowsyou to package your application along with its environment, ensuring that it runs consistently across different systems.

Creating a Docker Image

Here's a simple example of how to create a Dockerfile for a Go application:

```Dockerfile
# Use the official Golang image as a build stage FROM golang:1.19 AS build

WORKDIR /appCOPY . .

# Build the Go app
RUN go build -o myapp .

# Use a minimal base image for the final stage FROM alpine:latest

WORKDIR /root/
COPY --from=build /app/myapp .

# Expose the port and commandEXPOSE 8080
CMD ["./myapp"]
```

To build and run the Docker image:

```bash
# Build the Docker imagedocker build -t myapp .

# Run the Docker container docker run -p 8080:8080 myapp
```

Advantages of Using Docker

150

Isolation: Docker containers encapsulate everything your application needs to run, minimizing the risk of conflicts with other applications.
Scalability: Containers can be easily orchestrated using tools like Kubernetes, making it simple to scale your application in production environments.

4. Distribution through Package Managers

Another distribution approach is to create packages for various operating system package managers. For example, you can create `.deb` packages for Debian-based systems or `.rpm` for Red Hat-based systems.

Tools and Resources
FPM (Effing Package Management): A popular tool for packaging applications for various systems. It simplifies the creation of `.deb`, `.rpm`, and other package formats.

```bash
fpm -s dir -t deb ./myapp=/usr/local/bin/myapp
```

Homebrew: For macOS, consider submitting your application to Homebrew for easy installation by users.

5. Continuous Integration and Deployment

Automating your distribution process can save time and reduce errors. Using CI/CD pipelines with platforms like GitHub Actions, GitLab CI, or Travis CI can streamline your workflow. For example, you could create a pipeline that automatically builds and publishes your application each time a new version is tagged in your repository.

An Example Workflow with GitHub Actions
```yaml
name: Go Build and Release

on:
push:
tags:
v*

jobs:
build:
runs-on: ubuntu-lateststeps:
name: Checkout
uses: actions/checkout@v2

name: Set up Go
uses: actions/setup-go@v2with:
go-version: '1.19'
```

name: Buildrun: |
go build -o myapp

name: Publish
uses: softprops/action-gh-release@v1with:
tag_name: ${{ github.ref }}files: myapp
env:
GITHUB_TOKEN: ${{ secrets.GITHUB_TOKEN }}

Distributing your Go applications effectively involves understanding various packaging methods, leveraging the cross-compilation capabilities, and utilizing modern tools for streamlined processes. Whether you're distributing binaries, creating Docker images, or utilizing package managers, choosing the right approach depends on your target audience and deployment scenarios.

Introduction to Distributed Systems in Go

Go, also known as Golang, has emerged as a popular programming language for developing distributed systems due to its simplicity, concurrency support, and performance. In this chapter, we will explore the foundational concepts of distributed systems, the reasons for using Go in building them, and the key characteristics that define a robust distributed architecture.

What is a Distributed System?

A distributed system is a model in which components located on networked computers communicate and coordinate their actions by passing messages. The components are often spread across multiple locations, yet they appear to the user as a single cohesive system. Key examples include cloud-based services, microservices architectures, and peer-to-peer platforms.

Key Characteristics of Distributed Systems

Scalability: Distributed systems can be scaled horizontally by adding more machines or instances to manage increased load, making them suitable for applications with varying demand.

Fault Tolerance: A properly designed distributed system can continue to operate even when some of its components fail. This is achieved through redundancy and data replication.

Concurrency: Distributed systems allow for multiple processes to execute simultaneously across different nodes, improving overall throughput.

Transparency: An ideal distributed system should hide its complexity from the user, providing seamless interaction as if it were a single system.

Consistency: With multiple copies of data in a distributed system, ensuring data integrity and consistency becomes a challenge and is a key area of focus for developers.

Why Use Go for Distributed Systems?

Go was created by Google engineers Robert Griesemer, Rob Pike, and Ken Thompson, and it was designed with modern hardware and system software challenges in mind. Here are several reasons why Go is particularly well-suited for building distributed systems:

Concurrency Model: Go provides goroutines, which

are lightweight threads managed by the Go runtime. Goroutines allow developers to write concurrent code easily, making it simple to manage multiple tasks simultaneously—this is essential in distributed systems.

Performance: Go is a compiled language, and its performance is comparable to that of lower-level languages like C and C++. This efficiency is crucial in systems that require high throughput and low latency.

Simplicity and Readability: The syntax and design of Go promote writing clean, simple, and maintainable code. This is particularly beneficial in large teams working on complex distributed systems.

Rich Standard Library: Go comes with a robust standard library that provides many features useful for distributed systems, including support for HTTP, JSON handling, and various networking protocols.

Built-in Testing and Profiling: Go's built-in testing framework and profiling tools make it easier to build reliable systems and identify bottlenecks during development.

Components of a Distributed System

When designing a distributed system, certain components are essential:

Nodes: The individual machines or instances that participate in the system.

Communication Protocols: The rules and conventions for data exchange between nodes. Common protocols include HTTP, gRPC, and message brokers like Kafka.

Data Storage: Depending on the application, data can be stored in databases (SQL or NoSQL), file systems, or object storage services.

Load Balancers: These are used to distribute traffic across multiple nodes, ensuring no single component becomes a bottleneck.

Service Registry and Discovery: In service-oriented architectures, keeping track of service locations and instances is crucial for inter-service communication.

Monitoring and Logging: To ensure system health and performance, comprehensive monitoring and logging tools should be in place.

Challenges in Distributed Systems

Building distributed systems is not without its challenges. Developers must contend with:

Network Reliability: Networks can be unpredictable, and message loss can occur. Robust error handling and retries are essential.

Latency: Communication between nodes introduces latency. Designing the system to reduce round-trip times is critical.

Data Consistency: Achieving strong consistency across distributed components can be complex, often requiring consensus algorithms like Raft or Paxos.

Security: Protecting data in transit and at rest, along with ensuring secure communication between nodes, is vital.

Debugging and Testing: The complexity of distributed systems can make debugging more challenging than in traditional monolithic systems.

The combination of Go's concurrency model, performance, simplicity, and extensive libraries makes it an attractive choice for developers tackling the challenges inherent in building distributed systems. As we progress through this book, we will delve deeper into practical applications of these principles, culminating in the development of a complete distributed system leveraging the capabilities of Go.

Building a Distributed Cache with Go

In modern web applications, where speed and efficiency are crucial, implementing a distributed cache can significantly enhance performance by reducing the load on databases and accelerating data retrieval times. This chapter will guide you through the process of building a simple distributed cache using Go, one of the most popular programming languages known for its speed and efficiency.

Understanding Caching

Before diving into implementation, it's essential to understand the concept of caching. A cache is a temporary storage area that holds copies of frequently accessed data. By storing this data in a cache, subsequent requests can be served much faster than if they had to retrieve the data from the original source(e.g., a database).

Types of Caches

In-Memory Caches: These caches store data in the server's memory, making access extremely fast. Examples include Redis and Memcached.

Disk-Based Caches: These caches use storage disks to persist data, offering more significant storage capacity but slower access times.

Distributed Caches: These caches span multiple servers, providing redundancy and scalability. They are particularly useful for large applications that need to handle vast amounts of data across multiple nodes.

Why Go?

Go, also known as Golang, was developed at Google and is designed for high-performance concurrent programming. Its simple syntax, robust standard library, and built-in support for concurrency make it an excellent choice for building distributed systems. Go's goroutines allow for lightweight concurrent operations, making it suitable for handling multiple cache operations simultaneously.

Setting Up the Environment

Before we start coding, ensure you have the following prerequisites installed:

Go (version 1.16 or higher)
A working development environment (IDE or text editor)
Basic understanding of Go's syntax and concurrency model ## Designing the Cache
Let's design a simple distributed cache with the following features:

Get: Retrieve a value by key.
Set: Store a value by key.
Invalidate: Remove a key from the cache.
Expiration: Automatically remove items after a certain period. ### Architecture Overview Our distributed cache will consist of multiple nodes, where each node holds a portion of the cached data. The nodes will communicate over a network using a simple protocol to facilitate data storage and retrieval. Here are the key components:

Node: Each node will hold cache data and provide methods for cache operations.
Client: The client will handle requests and route them to the appropriate node.
Data Store: A lightweight in-memory key-value store for caching. ## Implementing the Cache
Now, let's dive into the implementation part. ### Step 1: Define the Cache Data Structure
We'll start by defining the data structure for our cache.

```go
package main

import ("sync"
"time"
)

type CacheItem struct {Value    interface{}    Expiration
int64
}

type Node struct {sync.RWMutex
items map[string]CacheItem
}

func NewNode() *Node {return &Node{
items: make(map[string]CacheItem),
}
}
```

Step 2: Implement Set and Get Methods

Next, we'll implement methods for setting and getting cache items.

```go
func (n *Node) Set(key string, value interface{}, duration
time.Duration) {n.Lock()
defer n.Unlock()

expiration   :=   time.Now().Add(duration).UnixNano()
```
160

```go
n.items[key] = CacheItem{
Value: value, Expiration: expiration,

}
}

func (n *Node) Get(key string) (interface{}, bool) {
n.RLock()
defer n.RUnlock()

item, found := n.items[key]
if !found || time.Now().UnixNano() > item.Expiration {
return nil, false
}
return item.Value, true
}
```

Step 3: Implement Invalidation

To ensure that we can remove items from the cache, we'll implement the Invalidate method.

```go
func (n *Node) Invalidate(key string) {n.Lock()
defer n.Unlock() delete(n.items, key)
}
```

Step 4: Handle Expiration

To handle expiration of cache items, we can create a goroutine that checks for expired items periodically.

161

```go
func (n *Node) cleanup() {
ticker := time.NewTicker(time.Minute)go func() {
for {
<-ticker.Cn.Lock()
for key, item := range n.items {
if    time.Now().UnixNano()    >    item.Expiration    {
delete(n.items, key)
}
}
n.Unlock()
}
}()
}
```

Step 5: Communication Between Nodes

We'll leverage HTTP for communication between nodes. Each node will expose an HTTP API for clientinteraction.

```go
import (
"encoding/json""net/http"
)

func (n *Node) ServeHTTP(w http.ResponseWriter, r *http.Request) {switch r.Method {
case http.MethodPost:var req struct {
Key string    `json:"key"` Value interface{} `json:"value"`
TTL int64    `json:"ttl"` // Time to live in seconds
}
if err := json.NewDecoder(r.Body).Decode(&req); err !=
```

```go
nil {http.Error(w, err.Error(), http.StatusBadRequest)
return
}
n.Set(req.Key,                          req.Value,
time.Duration(req.TTL)*time.Second)
w.WriteHeader(http.StatusNoContent)

case http.MethodGet:
key  :=  r.URL.Query().Get("key")  if val,  found  :=
n.Get(key); found {
json.NewEncoder(w).Encode(val)
} else {
http.Error(w, "Not found", http.StatusNotFound)
}

case http.MethodDelete:
key  :=  r.URL.Query().Get("key")  n.Invalidate(key)
w.WriteHeader(http.StatusNoContent)

default:
http.Error(w,        "Method        Not        Allowed",
http.StatusMethodNotAllowed)
}
}
```

Step 6: Running the Node

Finally, we need to set up the HTTP server to listen for requests.

```go
func main() {
```

```
node := NewNode() node.cleanup() http.Handle("/",
node)
http.ListenAndServe(":8080", nil) // Run the server on
port 8080
}
```

Testing the Distributed Cache

To test our distributed cache system, you can use tools like
`curl`, Postman, or write a simple client in Go. The
following example demonstrates how to test using `curl`
commands:

Set a value:
```bash
curl -X POST -H "Content-Type: application/json" -d
'{"key": "foo", "value": "bar", "ttl": 60}'
http://localhost:8080
```

Get a value:
```bash
curl "http://localhost:8080?key=foo"
```

Invalidate a value:
```bash
curl -X DELETE "http://localhost:8080?key=foo"
```

In this chapter, we explored how to build a simple
distributed cache in Go. We covered the fundamental

concepts of caching, designed the cache architecture, and implemented a basic HTTP-based distributed cache.

Conclusion

As we reach the end of this journey through system programming with Go, it's important to reflect on the knowledge and skills you've acquired along the way. You've delved into the intricacies of system calls, explored the fundamentals of networking, and built a strong foundation in security practices—all while creating practical Golang projects that reinforce these concepts.

Go is not just a programming language; it's a powerful tool that enables you to interact with the underlying operating system, optimize performance, and build robust applications. By mastering system programming with Go, you are well-equipped to tackle real-world challenges, streamline system-level tasks, and heighten your understanding of how software interacts with hardware.

Beyond technical skills, you've also developed a mindset geared toward problem-solving and innovation. The projects we explored together demonstrate how you can leverage Go's capabilities to create efficient solutions, whether it's implementing network protocols, managing concurrent tasks, or enhancing application security. Each line of code not only serves a functional purpose but also reflects your growing expertise and creative approach to system programming.

We encourage you to continue experimenting with your newfound skills. The world of system programming is vast and constantly evolving. Engage with the community, contribute to open-source projects, and stay updated on the latest advancements in Go and system-level programming. Your journey doesn't end here; it's merely the beginning of a lifelong exploration that can lead to remarkable opportunities in the tech industry.

Thank you for joining us on this educational adventure. We hope this ebook has not only enlightened you about system programming in Go but has also inspired you to unleash your creativity and pursue your passions in technology. Keep coding, keep learning, and most importantly, keep exploring the limitless possibilities that await you!

Biography

Tommy Clark is a passionate and dynamic author who combines a deep love for technology with an insatiable curiosity for innovation. As the mastermind behind the book *"Clark: A Journey Through Expertise and Innovation,"* Tommy brings years of hands-on experience in web development, web applications, and system administration to the forefront, offering readers a unique and insightful perspective.

With a strong background in Go programming and an ever-evolving fascination with crafting robust, efficient systems, Tommy excels at turning complex technical concepts into practical, actionable strategies. Whether building cutting-edge web solutions or diving into the intricate details of system optimization, Tommy's expertise is both broad and profound.

When not immersed in coding or writing, Tommy enjoys exploring the latest tech trends, tinkering with open-source projects, and mentoring aspiring developers. His enthusiasm for technology and dedication to empowering others shine through in everything he creates.

Join Tommy Clark on this exciting journey to unlock the full potential of technology—and get ready to be inspired, informed, and equipped to tackle your next big challenge!

Glossary: System Programming with Go

A

API (Application Programming Interface)
A set of rules and protocols for building and interacting with software applications. In Go, APIs often define how different components of a program should interact, governing the requests and responses between them.

Affinity
The relationship between a process and a specific processor or core. In system programming, managing processor affinity can improve performance by reducing context switching and cache misses.

C

Concurrent Programming

167

A programming paradigm that allows multiple processes or threads to run simultaneously. Go has built-in support for concurrency through goroutines and channels.

Context
An abstraction in Go that carries deadlines, cancellation signals, and other request-scoped values across API boundaries. It is essential for managing the lifecycle of requests and resources.

Channel
A Go primitive used for communication between goroutines. Channels allow for the safe transfer of data and synchronization between concurrent processes.

D

Deadlock
A situation in concurrent programming where two or more goroutines are unable to proceed because each is waiting for the other to release resources. Understanding and avoiding deadlocks is critical for robust system programming.

Dispatch
The process of sending tasks to be executed, often in the context of managing goroutines and scheduling their execution in Go.

E

Escape Analysis
Go's compiler feature that determines whether a variable

is allocated on the stack or the heap. This analysis is crucial for optimizing memory usage and performance in Go applications.

F

Goroutine
A lightweight thread managed by the Go runtime. Goroutines are a core feature of Go's concurrency model, allowing developers to run functions concurrently with minimal overhead.

Function Closure
A technique in Go where a function is defined within another function, allowing the inner function to access the outer function's variables. Closures are powerful for creating flexible and reusable code.## G
Go Modules
A dependency management system in Go that simplifies the inclusion and versioning of external libraries. It allows developers to manage dependencies efficiently across various projects.

Garbage Collection
An automatic memory management feature in Go that recycles memory that is no longer in use. Understanding garbage collection's impact on performance is vital for system programmers.

I

Interface
A Go type that specifies a contract of methods a struct

must implement. Interfaces allow for polymorphism and enable flexibility in code design.

IPC (Inter-Process Communication)
Methods and techniques used for communication between different processes. Go provides several libraries and tools for IPC, including channels and shared memory.

L

Lock
A synchronization primitive used to control access to a shared resource in concurrent programming. Go provides mutexes as a way to implement locking.

M

Mutex (Mutual Exclusion)
A locking mechanism that restricts access to a resource to only one goroutine at a time, preventing data races in concurrent applications.

Memory Leak
A situation where a program consumes memory but fails to release it after usage. In system programming, avoiding memory leaks is crucial for maintaining efficient resource use.

P

Piping
A method for passing output from one program or process directly as input to another. Go provides interfaces for

piping data between goroutines and functions seamlessly.

Process
An instance of a running program. In the context of system programming, understanding how to manage processes is essential for performance and resource management.

R

Race Condition
A situation in concurrent programming where the outcome depends on the timing of events, leading to unpredictable behavior. Go provides tools to detect race conditions, such as the `go run -race` flag.

Runtime
The Go runtime is responsible for managing goroutines, memory allocation, and garbage collection. Understanding the runtime is key to optimizing Go applications.

S

Scheduler
The component of the Go runtime that manages the execution of goroutines, deciding when and where they run on available processors.

System Call
A request made by a program to the operating system's kernel. System calls allow programs to perform operations like file manipulation, process control, and networking.

T

Thread
A unit of execution within a process. While goroutines are managed by the Go runtime, threads may still play a role when Go interacts with system-level operations.

Type Assertion
A way to retrieve the dynamic type of an interface variable in Go. Type assertions are indispensable for working with interfaces and ensuring type safety.

U

Uptime
The amount of time a system has been up and running without interruption. Monitoring uptime is essential in system programming for assessing system reliability.

Utility Package
A collection of functions and routines that provide common functionalities across various applications. Go's standard library includes many utility packages that simplify system programming tasks.